# HISTORY OF THE INTERNATIONAL POLITICAL SCIENCE ASSOCIATION 1949-1999

D1491225

## John Coakley and John Trent

International Political Science Association
2000

Ordering information

Copies of this publication may be ordered from the
International Political Science Association
Department of Politics, University College Dublin
Belfield, Dublin 4, Ireland
fax: +353-1-706 17171
email: ipsa@ucd.ie
http://www.ucd.ie/~ipsa

ISBN 1-902277-28-7

# CONTENTS

# LIST OF TABLES

# LIST OF FIGURES

# PREFACE

In this superb documentary, I can find only one fault. It is entirely too modest. IPSA was a product of the Cold War. The Cold War was a power struggle but also a war of ideas, and in that war IPSA was one of the earliest efforts (possibly the first) to transcend bipolar power alignments with its embrace of an organized, institutionalized, professionalized, indeed routinized commitment to inquiry itself, wherever it may lead. Virtually hidden on page 15 is a quote from Unesco's reasoning for making political science its first choice for evaluation leading to an experiment in an international scholarly discipline:

> ... Unesco's fundamental purpose [is] maintenance of peace through intellectual cooperation .... [T]he present tension between nations ... is tied closely to phenomena that political science should know and understand ... Whether or not today's education pierces the fog concealing the truth of political phenomena, it is the particular duty of political scientists to disperse that fog ....

Forty years of IPSA's 50-year history were deeply problematic for pursuit of "Unesco's fundamental purpose," because the war of ideas became a war of ideologies. The organized professional academic disciplines, led by IPSA, helped keep the idea of ideas alive. We need make no claim for important breakthroughs of knowledge or settlements of issues of war and peace. It was our job to maintain the search and extend the capacity for search and contention. Our success was our survival, persistence and dogged, diligent inquiry. In 18 Congresses and countless Research Committee panels and workshops, thousands of political scientists presented hundreds of thousands of research results. Many were called and few were chosen. Still fewer have been great. But organized scholarship—organized disciplines—are like democracy. To the very largest extent, the process is the purpose. As long as IPSA keeps the faith, greatness will take care of itself.

Compared to the first 50 years chronicled in the Coakley/Trent account, the second 50 ought to be a triumphant cake-walk.

*Theodore J Lowi*
*President, International Political Science Association*
*July 2000*

# FOREWORD

IPSA's fiftieth anniversary is an appropriate time to undertake a retrospective review of the development and achievements of the International Political Science Association. We are fortunate that in doing so we were not obliged to start from scratch. In 1969 the association published a twenty-year retrospective account, compiled by secretary general André Philippart and entitled *Association internationale de science politique: rapport de synthèse sur les 20 ans d'activité de l'association 1949-1969*. An update covering the period 1970-76 was compiled by Michèle Scohy for internal circulation, and in the late 1980s then Secretary General John Trent and his assistant, Dominique Bastien, completed a further stage in updating the Philippart volume and in incorporating additional material. Parts of this were used by the present secretary general as the basis for a series of articles that appeared during 1999 in the association's bulletin, *Participation*.

The present text is a substantially revised version of the articles that appeared in *Participation*, with additional textual material and appendices. We are indebted to many colleagues for assistance in preparing the text. We have borrowed the broad structure of this book from the original publication of André Philippart, without whose work much of the early history of the association would have been lost. The compilation of material dealing with the later period owes much to the record keeping of the late Francesco Kjellberg, secretary general 1988-94, and to a succession of able administrators: Liette Boucher in Ottawa, Lise Fog in Oslo and Louise Delaney and Margaret Brindley in Dublin. We are also grateful for the help of Michelle Murphy and Nuala Ryan of the IPSA office.

We are also grateful for comments to the current members of the IPSA executive committee. We are especially indebted to a number of colleagues who have read some or all of the text: to Asher Arian, Klaus von Beyme, Robert E Goodin, Serge Hurtig, Hans-Dieter Klingemann, Jean Laponce, Theodore J Lowi, Richard L Merritt and Guillermo O'Donnell. Precisely because of this debt and because of the fact that this book is being issued under the auspices of the association, the usual disclaimer applies with unusual force: errors of fact and interpretation are those of the authors.

*John Coakley and John Trent*
*Dublin and Ottawa*
*July 2000*

# 1 / INTRODUCTION

The twentieth century has been described as "the century of the social sciences", in that it was in this era that this particular branch of knowledge attained full intellectual maturity and broad political and institutional recognition.[1] The last years of the century indeed provided an occasion for major stock-taking overviews of developments within the various social sciences.[2] The international celebrations to mark the end of the century and of the second millennium coincided with a landmark also in the life of the International Political Science Association (IPSA). In the Autumn of 1999 the association marked its fiftieth birthday, and its Quebec congress in August 2000 is the fiftieth anniversary of the very first IPSA congress. It is an appropriate time to take stock of the history of this major international scholarly body and to assess its contribution to the evolution of organised political science in the second half of the twentieth century.

It is, of course, all too easy for those concerned with managing the infrastructure of academic activity to exaggerate the centrality of the formal institutions for which they are responsible. It has been clear since the time of Plato and Aristotle that while academies and organised groups may provide employment and stimulate enquiry they are not a necessary condition of intellectual progress. The study of politics can and will proceed even in the absence of such bodies. Yet, it is also clear that the investigation of political life will be conducted much more productively if it is actively encouraged within a framework that provides stable forums for discussion, facilitates intellectual contact and exchange, and offers a structured outlet through which research results may be brought to the attention of a wider audience.

The modest objective of this publication is to describe and assess IPSA's contribution over the past 50 years to the global advancement of political science. We can only do this by considering the association in the context

---

[1] Peter Wagner, "The twentieth century — the century of the social sciences?", pp. 16-41 in Ali Kazancigil and David Makinson, eds, *World social science report 1999* (Paris: Unesco Publishing / Elsevier, 1999).

[2] See, for example, Jennifer Platt, *A brief history of the ISA: 1948-1997* (Madrid: International Sociological Association, 1998)

of the intellectual and organisational evolution of the discipline and of the growth and consolidation of professional scholarly bodies of two types — the national political science associations that had a direct interest in the creation of IPSA, and the international academic unions that acted as models. This broader context is considered in the rest of this chapter. The remaining chapters examine in turn IPSA's organisational development, the growth of its membership and its efforts to cater to the needs of this membership by organising scientific meetings, promoting research and publishing the output of such research.

It should be stressed that neither IPSA nor any of its fellow-bodies among the list of international scholarly federations can claim a monopoly in terms of their contribution to international scholarship within their respective fields. The present publication is not intended to assert IPSA's precedence over other organisations in the promotion of the scholarly endeavour. Indeed, our starting point should be precisely the academic and organisational context within which IPSA came into being in 1949. Four features of this context stand out, and we will consider them in turn: the intellectual development of the discipline itself, the organisational evolution of political science within the university sector, the growth of national professional bodies to represent the discipline, and the appearance of international scholarly federations.

### The evolution of the discipline of political science

Histories of political science are not slow to highlight the discipline's ancient roots. The various editions of George Sabine's classic *History of political theory*, for instance, devote most of their space to the period 1500-1900, but the rest of the book is accounted for principally by the ancient and medieval periods rather than by the twentieth century.[3] Even when we extend outside the boundaries of political thought and consider the empirical study of political phenomena, the profound legacy of antiquity is clear: a recent succinct and authoritative overview of the history of political science predictably begins with Plato and Aristotle.[4]

Notwithstanding this impressive intellectual heritage and the profound impact of the political philosophical tradition, the growth of political sci-

[3] George Sabine, *A history of political theory*, 3rd ed. (London: George A Harrap, 1963); the first edition appeared in 1937 and the second in 1951.

[4] Gabriel A Almond, "Political science: the history of the discipline", pp. 50-96 in Robert E Goodin and Hans-Dieter Klingemann, eds, *A new handbook of political science* (Oxford: Oxford University Press, 1996).

ence of the kind with which we are now familiar is a distinctly modern development.[5] Well into the twentieth century, the discipline's identity remained insecure and its academic standing was subject to challenges of varying intensities in different parts of the world. By the late 1940s, the position of political science was still imperfectly established. A contemporary survey suggested that the various national traditions were clustered into five major groups:

• the American approach, characterised by an openness to methodologies from the other social sciences and especially psychology, now making a transition from institutionalism to behaviouralism (the USA, the Middle East and parts of Asia, such as China)

• the British approach, embedded in but slowly asserting its independence from moral philosophy (the United Kingdom and most Commonwealth countries, including India)

• the French approach, rooted in the Roman law tradition (France, Mediterranean Europe and Latin America)

• the German approach, originating in constitutional and administrative law and evolving into the systematic study of the state (Germany, Austria and certain adjacent countries such as the Netherlands and Scandinavia, and Japan)

• the Soviet approach, characterised by the marxist-leninist mode of analysis and comprising essentially a branch of sociology, rooted in political economy (the Soviet Union and other countries moving under communist influence).[6]

While this typology, like most generalisations, represents an oversimplification of reality, it has a particular significance that arises from the cir-

---

[5] Discussion of the literature would be out of place here, but in addition to other works cited here, a number of lively reviews of the history of the discipline — and reviews of these reviews — have appeared; for extended and remarkably complementary examples of the latter, see James Farr, "The history of political science", *American journal of political science* 32 (4), 1988, pp. 1175-95; John S Dryzek and Stephen T Leonard, "History and discipline in political science", *American political science review* 82 (4), 1988, pp. 1245-60; and Yves Viltard, "Faire l'histoire de la science politique n'est pas neutre: à propos de *Political science in history*", *Revue française de science politique* 49 (1), 1999, pp. 123-35, which itself focuses heavily on James Farr, John S Dryzek and Stephen T Leonard, eds, *Political science in history: research programs and political traditions* (Cambridge: Cambridge University Press, 1995).

[6] Massimo Salvadori, "The Unesco project: methods in political science", pp. 1-20 in Unesco, *Contemporary political science: a survey of methods, research and teaching* (Paris: Unesco, 1950), pp. 7-9; and Masamichi Royama, "Political science in Japan", pp. 313-22 in *ibid*, pp. 314-5, 318.

cumstances in which it was arrived at (see pp. 15-16). It is clear that there were even then very large variations within most of the national groups identified. Examples could be multiplied, but if we confine ourselves to early IPSA activists it would be difficult to see Kenneth Wheare and Maurice Duverger as conforming comfortably to what are described here as the characteristics of the British and French traditions respectively; neither does this typology take account of the tradition of political geography in France, as represented by André Siegfried, nor of the inheritance of Max Weber in German political sociology. By contrast, the Soviet approach is credited with a place in the discipline which, though it appropriately anticipated IPSA's inclusive perspective on the boundaries of the discipline, was later questioned by many political scientists.

Since the 1950s, global convergence and rapid disciplinary development have been outstanding features of the history of political science. David Easton's classification of the stages through which American political science passed from the nineteenth century to the 1960s had a wider applicability; indeed, it is probable that some of the approaches whose eras of dominance have long passed in the United States continued to enjoy significant influence in other parts of the world well into the latter part of the twentieth century. These were *universalism*, the study of politics as part of universal moral philosophy; *legalism*, the study of the state as essentially a legal structure (and thus focusing on the study of constitutions and legal norms); *realism*, with an emphasis on the actual practice of political life rather than on formal structures; and *behaviouralism*, with its emphasis on a new form of reality, to be grasped not just by the study of institutions but also by utilising insights from other disciplines such as psychology and sociology.[7] More recent analyses would, of course, draw attention to a range of post-behaviouralist approaches and, indeed, to alternative perspectives on the history of the discipline.[8]

It is thus likely that the path of evolution of American political science charted a route for the discipline in other parts of the world. A benchmark review of world political science at the beginning of the 1980s noted the fact that political scientists were still overwhelmingly concentrated in

---

[7] David Easton, "Political science", pp. 282-98 in *International encyclopedia of the social sciences* (London: Macmillan, 1968), vol. 12.

[8] See especially Almond, "Political science" (1996) and Gabriel Almond, "Separate tables: schools and sects in political science", pp. 13-31 in *A discipline divided: schools and sects in political science* (Newbury Park: Sage, 1990); and, for more detailed accounts, Ada W Finifter, *Political science: the state of the discipline II* (Washington, DC: American Political Science Association, 1993).

North America (where there were about 15-16,000 of them), with western
Europe trailing far behind (about 2,500) and the discipline seriously un-
derdeveloped in other parts of the world.[9] Nevertheless, it has been suggested that the social sciences in Europe, far from being an appendage to
the American social sciences, evolved in a distinctive pattern in the post-
war period, frequently following a path that was at variance with (or, indeed, a reaction to) developments in the United States.[10] In the case of political science, the institutional reaction against the United States may have
been all the more pronounced because of the extent of the intellectual debt:
European political science stole a march on the other social sciences with
the very early creation of a European political science community, in large
measure as part of an effort to assert European autonomy within the discipline. This derived in part from political circumstances associated with the
expansion and deepening of the European Community and the European
Union, but one of its earliest expressions arose from an initiative of far-
sighted European scholars. This was the launch of the inter-university
European Consortium for Political Research in 1970.[11]

This discussion of course illustrates the dominance of the West in the
evolution of political science, a feature that emerges clearly in the major
surveys of the discipline.[12] It should not be seen as excluding the possibil-
ity of distinctive variants on these approaches in certain countries, even if
non-western scholars like Ibn Khaldun are written out of standard histories of political science. Examples are the study of the ancient Hindu texts
in India and the traditional perception of political science as a branch of

[9] William G Andrews, "Introduction: freaks, rainbows and pots of gold", pp. 1-6 in William G Andrews, ed., *International handbook of political science* (Westport, CT: Greenwood
Press, 1982).

[10] Guido Martinotti, "The recovery of western European social sciences since 1945", pp.
84-91 in Kazancigil and Makinson, *World social science report* (1999).

[11] Kenneth Newton, "The European Consortium for Political Research", *European journal
of political research* 20 (3-4), 1991, pp. 445-58. For reports on the state of political science in
Europe in the period to 1996, see Marie-Françoise Durand and Jean-Louis Quermonne, eds,
*Political science in Europe — final report*, available http://www.epsnet.org/papers
/sommaire.htm#1 [2000-07-16]

[12] See Unesco, *Contemporary political science* (1950); Jan Barents, *Political science in western
Europe: a trend report* (London: Stevens, 1961); Dwight Waldo, "Political science: tradition,
discipline, profession, science, enterprise", pp. 1-130 in Fred I Greenstein and Nelson W
Polsby, eds *Handbook of political science* (Reading, MA: Addison-Wesley, 1975), vol. 1; An-
drews, *International handbook* (1982); David Easton, John G Gunnell and Luigi Graziano, eds
*The development of political science: a comparative survey* (London: Routledge, 1991); and
Goodin and Klingemann, *New handbook* (1996).

the feudal system of Confucianism in pre-Meiji Japan.[13] One eloquent study of political science in Nigeria evokes an image that must be reasonably representative of much of non-western political science: it depicts a discipline that is "a reproduction of dominant, expatriate political science" that attests to the pervasiveness of the colonial inheritance, in which fads and trends arrive either too late or in watered-down forms.[14]

Yet it would be unfair and inaccurate simply to regard the rest of the world as a passive recipient of wisdom from the west, and especially from North America. Although it may not loom large in the consciousness of western scholars, the reality is that a number of African and especially Latin American scholars have made major original contributions (many of them later picked up, critically or otherwise, by their American and European colleagues) in such areas as theory of the state, authoritarian states and regimes, transitions to democracy, political economy, political aspects of dependency and world systems. Especially in recent years, the Asian resurgence has extended well beyond the bounds of economics into the domain of social science research, and here, too, the significance of independent contributions in the areas of democratisation, political economy and globalisation should not be underestimated.

## Political science as an academic subject

Although the study of politics in a recognisably academic way thus predates by centuries the birth of the university in the west, the subject itself was slow to make its appearance on the curriculum.[15] Of the four faculties of the medieval university (theology, medicine, law and philosophy), at least two could be seen as embracing the study of government and political life (while this might be true of a third, theology, the evolution of that faculty did not in practice promote the formal study of political science).

The faculty of law of necessity extended to the study of institutions of government and their underpinning in statute and convention. In time, the study of principles of jurisprudence and of constitutional and administra-

---

[13] Angadipuram Appadorai, "Political science in India", pp. 38-47 in Unesco, *Contemporary political science* (1950), pp. 40-1; and Royama, "Political science in Japan", p. 313.

[14] L Adele Jinadu, "The institutional development of political science in Nigeria: trends, problems and prospects", *International political science review* 8 (1) 1987, pp. 59-72.

[15] It has been suggested that the study of politics in one form or another is "amongst the most venerable of academic pursuits", but that the idea of a department of politics as a normal university department is a relatively modern phenomenon—dating only from the second world war in the case of the United Kingdom; see FF Ridley, *The study of government: political science and public administration* (London: George Allen & Unwin, 1975), p. 14.

tive law evolved in some universities into the formal designation of politics as an area of study. Broadly speaking, there were two paths of development. In German-speaking central Europe "general state theory" (*allgemeine Staatslehre*) evolved at a relatively early stage from the study of law, and by no means in isolation from contemporary political events and needs. It eventually formed the core of the modern study of politics.[16] In France, as indeed in other countries adhering to the Roman law tradition, the study of political life was subordinated to that of law, and even though it might have advanced within other disciplines such as history and sociology, it was still in a state of undoubted underdevelopment by the middle of the twentieth century.[17] Indeed, the linkage between political science and law remained pronounced in much of the Latin world well into the latter part of the century, with a number of political science departments eventually asserting their independence of their parent, law, only in recent decades.[18]

The faculty of philosophy, with its traditionally all-embracing reach, constituted a second home for the study of politics. Yet here, too, the development of separate politics departments was slow. Instead, as the university developed and chairs in an increasingly diverse range of subjects were created, it was such disciplines as languages, mathematics and history that were first to achieve recognition. Even economics, sociology and anthropology made more rapid strides than political science in the nineteenth century. The study of politics thus tended to be seen as a branch of moral philosophy, though in some cases, such as Canada, there was an especially strong linkage with economics.[19] In yet another sense, a newer form of economics was home to that interpretation of political life that

---

[16] Ludwig Adamovich, "The science of the state in Germany and Austria", pp. 23-37 in Unesco, *Contemporary political science* (1950), pp. 23-31.

[17] Thus in the late 1940s Raymond Aron could argue emphatically that "in France there is no 'political science' in the singular"; see "Political science in France", pp. 48-64 in Unesco, *Contemporary political science* (1950), p. 50; see also Lazare Kopelmanas, "Teaching and organization of research in the field of political science in France", pp. 647-654 in *ibid*, p. 647.

[18] Notwithstanding this formal parentage, in a number of cases, as in certain Brazilian universities, political science evolved within philosophy faculties; see Djacir Menezes, "Political science in Brazil during the last thirty years", pp. 228-32 in Unesco, *Contemporary political science* (1950), p. 228.

[19] Burton S Keirstead and Frederick M Watkins, "Political science in Canada", pp. 171-7 in Unesco, *Contemporary political science* (1950), p. 171; Michael Stein and John E Trent, "Canada", pp. 34-46 in Andrews, *International handbook* (1982).

came to be known as "historical materialism", the characteristic path taken by the study of politics in communist-controlled countries.[20]

The history of the creation of politics departments reflects this pattern of retarded academic recognition of the autonomy of the discipline. It is true that the University of Leiden in the Netherlands began formal teaching of politics in 1613, and that professorships in the subject appeared shortly after this date.[21] Similarly, the University of Uppsala in Sweden created a chair of Discourse and Politics in 1622 and Åbo Akademi (then in Sweden, now in Finland) created a chair of Politics and History in 1640.[22] But it would be difficult to argue that the concerns of professorships of these kinds had much in common with those of political science departments of the contemporary world.

The second half of the nineteenth century saw the emergence of embryonic political science departments. In part this arose from the foundation of new universities that sought to give recognition to what was seen as a modern and socially relevant subject. In Dublin, for instance the new Catholic University of Ireland (now University College Dublin) created a chair of "social and political science" in 1855; in a characteristically Catholic form, this was reborn as a department of "Ethics and politics" in 1908. From the 1840s onwards, "politics" began to acquire a more modern meaning in Uppsala.[23] Elsewhere in Sweden the development of the discipline got under way: a professorship of history and political science was created at Lund in 1889, and a professorship of political science was created in Gothenburg in 1901.[24] In Belgium, schools for political and social sciences were created at the Catholic University of Louvain and the Free University of Brussels in 1893.[25] In pre-war Germany and elsewhere in Europe, the study of political phenomena also made striking advances under other labels, such as that of sociology. But the reality is that the typical contemporary European political science department is essentially a twen-

---

[20] Adam Schaff and Stanislaw Ehrlich, "The concept of dialectical materialism in political science", pp. 326-36 in Unesco, *Contemporary political science* (1950).

[21] Hans Daalder, "Political science in the Netherlands", *European journal of political research* 20 (3-4), 1991, pp. 179-300.

[22] Dag Anckar, "Political science in the Nordic countries", *International political science review* 8 (1), 1987, pp. 73-84.

[23] Olof Ruin, "Sweden: research", pp. 219-319 in Andrews, *International handbook* (1982).

[24] Dag Anckar, "Nordic political science: trends, roles, approaches", *European journal of political research* 20 (3-4), 1991, pp.239-61.

[25] André P Frognier and L de Winter, "The state of political science in Belgium", *European journal of political research* 20 (3-4), 1991, pp. 389-97.

tieth century creation. Even at the end of the 1940s, there was still not a single department of politics in the United Kingdom.[26]

Although the growth of the discipline in American universities would quickly overshadow the pattern of development in Europe, there, too, politics tended to lag behind other subjects in terms of its formal recognition within the university system. It is instructive to recall the slow stages by which the discipline developed even in the United States: the inauguration of the first professorship of History and Political Science at Columbia in 1857; the creation of a Department of History, Social and Political Science at Cornell in 1868; the launch of the first graduate programme in Historical and Political Studies at Johns Hopkins in 1876; and the appearance of the first postgraduate School of Political Science at Columbia four years later. Separate departments of political science were established at Columbia (1903), Illinois and Wisconsin (1904) and Michigan (1911); by 1914, out of 531 colleges, 200 taught courses in political science and 40 had independent departments of political science.[27] This achievement was staggering by the standards of Europe, the global region that most closely resembled the United States in terms of the development of the discipline.

Finally, it is important to recall that the formal study of political science could also follow an alternative academic path to the university route. While the academic study of politics might be of great interest to professors and of some interest to the general public, the study of the operation of the state and its organs was of practical significance for public office holders. It is thus not surprising that the nineteenth century fascination with the need for practical knowledge led to the creation of educational institutions with a significant training function. It was in this spirit that the Ecole Libre des Sciences Politiques was created in Paris in 1872 (to be succeeded in 1945 by the Fondation Nationale des Sciences Politiques and the Institut d'Etudes Politiques, Paris). The London School of Economics and Political Science (LSE) was founded in 1895 on this model, and these two schools themselves became models for later institutions of the same kind in other countries — for example, the Ecole des Sciences Sociales et Politiques at Lausanne, 1902; the Deutsche Hochschule für Politik in Berlin, 1920; and the School for Politics and Social Problems (later the Prague School of Eco-

---

[26] George DH Cole, "The study of politics in British universities", pp. 617-46 in Unesco, *Contemporary political science* (1950), p. 617

[27] David M Ricci, *The tragedy of political science: politics, scholarship, and democracy* (New Haven: Yale University Press, 1984), pp. 59-61.

nomics) in Prague in the late 1940s.[28] LSE's concern for the "five Es" (education, economics, efficiency, equality and empire) appropriately summarised the spirit of the age, but, like its counterpart in Paris, LSE's area of concern extended over the whole range of the social sciences rather than focusing on political science in the modern sense.[29]

## National political science associations

The third context that needs to be considered in reviewing the history of IPSA is that of the national political science associations that have had such an important bearing on its evolution—a consideration that derives even more importance from the fact that IPSA's identity as a federation of national associations has been a long-standing feature. These associations may be placed in two groups, those that pre-dated IPSA and contributed to its foundation, and those that appeared afterwards as national or regional organisations of scholars, most of them also entering into formal relations with IPSA, and several of them owing their very creation to support from IPSA.

Before the second world war, the slow pace of development of political science was reflected in the even more hesitant steps in the direction of the formation of national professional associations of political scientists. Indeed, in most countries there was simply no organisation for university-based political scientists. In such cases, alternative media for structured contact between academic analysts of political life may well have existed. One model is that of the policy-oriented group, such as the left-leaning Fabian Society (1884) and the more conservative Political and Economic Planning (1931) in Great Britain.[30] It is also worth noting the existence even at this early stage of other institutions with an interest in the discipline, such as the Australian Institute of Political Science (1932).[31] A second forum was the broad academic association that included political scientists

---

[28] Ulrich Klöti, "Political science in Switzerland", European journal of political research 20 (3-4), 1991, pp. 413-24; Hans Kastendiek, "Political development and political science in West Germany", International political science review 8 (1), 1987, pp. 25-40; Jan Škaloud, "The organisation of political science in the Czech Republic", Participation 19 (2), 1995, pp. 4-5.

[29] Ralf Dahrendorf, LSE: a history of the London School of Economics and Political Science, 1895-1995 (Oxford: Oxford University Press, 1995).

[30] William A Robson, "Political science in Great Britain", pp. 294-312 in Unesco, Contemporary political science (1950), pp. 311-2. The latter body was reconstituted in 1978 to form the Policy Studies Institute.

[31] Colin Tatz and Graeme Starr, "Australia", pp. 74-84 in Andrews, International handbook (1982).

as a minority: the Vienna Jurists' Society (dating from the interwar period) is an example.[32] A third model is the once-off academic meeting. Examples are the political science congress held in Paris in 1900,[33] and the Scandinavian Political Science Congress held in Stockholm around 1930.[34]

The small number of national political science associations that predated IPSA therefore constitutes a rather striking list. It is headed by the American Political Science Association (1903), and includes also the Finnish Political Science Association (1935) and the Indian Political Science Association (1938). To these may be added the Canadian Political Science Association, which began life as an interdisciplinary body (1913) but which later (1968) became a purely political science association. Political turmoil had dealt a serious blow to the interwar Chinese Association of Political Science (1932), but postwar reconstruction facilitated the emergence of new associations in Japan (1948) and France (1949).

The intellectual ferment of the post-war period and a growing perception of the need for national organisation as a basis for international collaboration led to a mushrooming of national political science associations. Some appeared, as we have seen, just before the birth of IPSA. Others followed quickly thereafter: the Dutch, Israeli, Pakistani, Polish, Swedish, Swiss and United Kingdom associations (1950); the Austrian, Belgian, German and Hellenic associations (1951); and the Australasian, Brazilian and Italian associations (1952). Organisations in communist-governed countries tended to come later: in Yugoslavia (1954), the Soviet Union (1960), Czechoslovakia (1964), and Bulgaria, Hungary and Romania (1968). Of course, the Polish association had existed already since 1950. Throughout the communist-controlled world the legitimacy of the discipline was qualitatively enhanced by the IPSA world congress in Moscow in 1979.

In addition to the associations mentioned, many of which were founded thanks to IPSA's initiative, national political science associations appeared elsewhere, though not all of them were to endure. A number of regional associations also emerged in due course. Two of these, the African Association of Political Science (1973) and the Asian-Pacific Political Science Association (dating from about 1983), became collective members of IPSA. Others, such as the Scandinavian Political Science Association (a loose um-

---

[32] Ludwig Adamovich, "The sciences of the state as taught in Austria", pp. 605-16 in Unesco, *Contemporary political science* (1950), p. 611.

[33] Jean Laponce, "Notes in search of a paper to commemorate the fiftieth anniversary of IPSA", *Participation* 24 (1), 2000, pp. 4-7.

[34] Elis Håstad, "Swedish political science", pp. 150-94 in Unesco, *Contemporary political science*, p. 151.

brella body) and the European Consortium for Political Research (1970) remain outside IPSA's formal ambit.

## International scholarly federations

The fourth important context within which IPSA emerged was the gradual move towards the establishment of global academic associations, a process that accelerated markedly in the immediate postwar years.[35] The model for these was provided by the various bodies that appeared in the natural sciences, or in disciplines with a significant natural science component. These early bodies were typically composed of individual members and were characterised by the practical nature of their declared aims. Examples close to the social sciences were the International Statistical Institute (1885) and the International Congress of Psychology (1889); and during the interwar period appeared the International Union for the Scientific Study of Population (1928) and the International Union of Administrative Sciences (1930).[36]

Although it was to devote special attention to political science (see chapter 2), Unesco also played a major role in promoting international collaboration and encouraging the formation of international scholarly federations in other disciplines. This followed from the ambition of Unesco's first Director-General, Julian Huxley, to advance the social as well as the natural sciences by endorsing a large number of autonomous programmes.[37] As well as political science, Unesco targeted economics, sociology and comparative law in 1949, and social psychology in 1950. There duly appeared the International Economic Association (1949), the International Sociological Association (1949), the International Association of Legal Science (1950) and the transformed International Union of Psychological Science (1951).

Unesco did not confine itself to the promotion of cross-national contact; it also strove to encourage interdisciplinary communication. To this end, once the number of international scholarly federations had reached a particular critical mass, it moved to set up a coordinating body for the social sciences. The outcome was the appearance in 1952 of an organisation that

[35] Jean Meynaud, "International cooperation in the field of social science", pp. 7-9 in Unesco, Reports and papers in the social sciences no. 5, 1956.

[36] TH Marshall, "International cooperation in the social sciences", pp. 9-14 in Unesco, Reports and papers in the social sciences no. 21, 1964.

[37] James P Sewell, Unesco and world politics: engaging in international relations (Princeton: Princeton University Press, 1975), pp. 113-7.

links the main international social science federations and that quickly came to represent Unesco's main channel for communication with them: the International Social Science Council.

It should not be assumed from this discussion that there existed an empty space for an international political science association into which IPSA could move without challenge. Indeed, we need to note the existence of two bodies that might, in other circumstances, have sought to redefine themselves with a view to occupying precisely the terrain that IPSA came to see as its own.

The first body was the International Institute of Differing Civilizations, a very energetic private body committed to the advancement of the "moral and political sciences"; its rather revealing full title was the International Institute of Political and Social Sciences in their Applications to Countries with Different Civilizations (INCIDI).[38] A clue to the institute's ethos is to be found in its original name on its foundation in 1894: the International Colonial Institute, an organisation that consisted of experts from countries with colonial empires and that enjoyed the support of colonial governments.[39]

The second body was the International Institute of Political and Constitutional History, founded in 1936 but renamed after the war the International Academy of Political Science and Constitutional History.[40] Although its vice chairmen included such distinguished comparativists as Crane Brinton and Boris Mirkine-Guetzévitch, and it consciously strove to present itself as focusing on mainstream political science, its roots clearly lay within the scholarly community of historians.

---

[38] "The International Institute of Differing Civilizations", in *International organizations in the social sciences, Unesco reports and papers in the social sciences* no. 5, 1956, pp. 40-42.

[39] "The International Institute of Political and Social Sciences in their Applications to Countries with Different Civilizations", *International social science bulletin*", 2 (3) 1950, pp. 378

[40] "The International Academy of Political Science and Constitutional History", *International social science bulletin*", 2 (3) 1950, pp. 378-9.

# 2 / ORGANISATIONAL DEVELOPMENT

While a thematic approach is adopted in considering IPSA's history in the rest of this volume, the present chapter deals with the institutional evolution of its basic machinery. This begins with the moment in which IPSA was formed—an episode in which the genetic make-up of the association was apparently definitively set. This is followed by a discussion of IPSA's fundamental rules—the constitution adopted in 1949 that has proven to be extraordinarily resilient. The rest of this chapter analyses the evolution of IPSA's main organs (the council, the executive committee and its subcommittees, the secretariat), and concludes with a discussion of the association's financial structure.

## The foundation of IPSA

If the broad context within which IPSA was conceived was the set of disciplinary and international scholarly developments discussed in the last chapter, the immediate circumstance was a remarkable conjunction of interests on the part of two partners—an ambitious and idealistic preoccupation with the grand goal of world peace on the part of the major global body charged with responsibility for education and science, the newly-created and youthfully vigorous Unesco, and a very precise and practical concern with the framework of the discipline on the part of an international group of far-seeing political scientists.

The first step towards the establishment of IPSA had modest beginnings within Unesco's Social Sciences Department. The department singled out political science as a discipline of exceptional importance, and the Unesco general assembly, meeting in Mexico City in November-December 1947, resolved as follows:

> 5.5 Methods in Political Science. The Director-General is instructed: to promote a study of the subject-matter and problems treated by political scientists of various countries in recent research materials (scientific publications and high-level text-books), the various types of approach and emphasis, the methods,

techniques and terminology employed and the quantity of production in recent political science...[1]

While the Social Sciences Department advanced a number of reasons for selecting political science, rather than any of the other social sciences, as its first choice for evaluation (including its underdevelopment, arising from its very recent origins, and the extent to which it lacked unity, due to its division into a range of national approaches), there was a more compelling reason. This deserves to be quoted more fully, since it was to constitute so central a place in the IPSA agenda and because it captures so vividly the atmosphere that informed IPSA's genesis:

> Another factor which points to the choice made by the Social Sciences Department is mentioned last, although it is the most important to civic groups and to Unesco's fundamental purpose: the maintenance of peace through intellectual cooperation. Among the many reasons why human beings have slaughtered one another, bringing untold sufferings (the most frightful are too recent to need description), some have been, and some are, purely political reasons. Whether these reasons are primary or secondary, the present tension between nations, and within many nations, is tied closely to phenomena that political scientists should know and understand. ... Whether or not today's education pierces the fog concealing the truth of political phenomena, it is the particular duty of political scientists to disperse that fog. Through this project on "Methods in Political Science", Unesco has tried to add a stone, however humble, to an important section of the complex edifice of human knowledge.[2]

The concrete outcome of the Unesco initiative was a very ambitious cross-national project led by William Ebenstein, professor of political science at Princeton University, USA, who began work in Unesco in February 1948. It was at this juncture that the commitment to this initiative of a large number of political scientists was mobilised. Political scientists from all parts of the world were invited to submit reports on political science within their countries, or on particular aspects of these, and to follow a rather detailed framework, grouped under three major sections covering content, methodology and terminology. In all, 84 reports were received, of which 51 were published. The reports reflected what was to become an enduring trend in the study of political science, and, indeed, in its partner social sciences. This was its exceptional strength in the west (53 reports were from Europe and 13 from North America, with only 18 from the rest of the world—five each from South America and the Middle East and four

---

[1] "The Unesco project: methods in political science", *International social science bulletin* 1 (1) 1949, p. 28.

[2] Ibid, pp. 28-29.

each from Asia and Oceania). On the other hand, efforts were already being made to maintain a geopolitical balance between blocs (12 came from countries where communist regimes had been or were being installed), and the dominant position of English was much less complete than it was later to become (38 papers were submitted in English, 31 in French, six in German, five in Spanish, three in Italian and one in Norwegian).[3]

Even before the reports saw the light of day in published form, another major development had taken place. This was an "unofficial" conference at Unesco House, Paris, in September 1948, to discuss various aspects of the project on methods. This event was the moment of conception of IPSA, and decisions taken at the meeting were of fundamental significance. Three of them merit further consideration since they had a lasting impact on the international organisation of political science.

The first was a clear articulation of the need for cross-national collaboration in the discipline, and a justification of this in terms of a particular intellectual imperative, one that was defined in a declaration approved by the conference:

> Political science evolves within national frameworks. In each country it has received the stamp of that country's particular historical traditions, educational mould, constitutional system, social structure and philosophical conceptions. These variations are in part justified. Every political scientist takes his problems and his directing ideas from the environment in which he lives. But for all that, it is still necessary for him to become aware of its peculiarities in order to avoid the twofold danger of isolation and prejudice. The goal of international co-operation in this sphere is not to replace the diversity of subjects dealt with and methods used by a single objective method. The juridical, historical, philosophical, sociological, psychological and statistical methods have all been successfully applied to the study of political ideas and institutions; on the other hand, the subjects studied differ greatly from country to country. The aim of co-operation is to help each political scientist to become acquainted with the developments of political science in other countries so as to broaden his horizon and facilitate mutual understanding.[4]

The second decision was essentially a definition of the parameters of the discipline and an effort to classify its subfields. It was agreed that the term "political science" (in the singular; in France and elsewhere the plural and more general expression "political sciences" was commonly used) was the

---

[3] Unesco, *Contemporary political science* (1950); these data are calculated from the list of reports on pp. 658-62.

[4] "The Unesco project: methods in political science", *International social science bulletin* 1 (1) 1949, pp. 29-30.

appropriate label for the discipline and, although the definition of "science" was left open, the domain of the "political" was seen as embracing a rather distinctive set of areas. These were defined and classified as follows:

  I. Political theory:
     1) political theory, 2) history of political ideas;
 II. Political institutions:
     1) the constitution, 2) central government, 3) regional and local government, 4) public administration, 5) economic and social functions of government, 6) comparative political institutions;
III. Parties, groups and public opinion:
     1) political parties, 2) groups and associations, 3) participation by the citizen in government and administration, 4) public opinion;
 IV. International relations:
     1) international policy, 2) international organization and administration, 3) international law.[5]

What is remarkable about this list is its longevity as a principle of organisation of the discipline within IPSA (and, indeed, in important respects outside it). It survives to the present, with minor modifications (notably, the insertion of a new first section on methods and a last section on national and area studies) as the classification system of the *International political science abstracts* (see chapter 6).

The third decision was the one with the most far-reaching practical consequences. It was agreed that a conference of political scientists be called in 1949 to launch an international political science association with a view to strengthening cultural ties within the discipline. A small preparatory committee was appointed to plan the conference in collaboration with Unesco. Its original members were Walter Sharp (USA, chair), John Goormaghtigh (Belgium, secretary), Raymond Aron (France) and William Robson (UK). To these were later added Angadipuram Appadorai (India) and Marcel Bridel (Switzerland).[6]

The prospects of the successful launch of the new association were greatly enhanced by a decision at Unesco's general conference in Beirut in December 1948 that the new Director-General should promote initiatives of this kind, and by a commitment to support them financially. The new Unesco Director-General, Jaime Torres Bodet, duly invited 23 specialists to Paris for the conference on 12-16 September 1949. The conference was presided over by Raymond Aron as chair, with William Robson and Quincy

---

[5] Ibid, p. 30.

[6] "International political science conference 1949", *International social science bulletin* 1 (1) 1949, pp. 66-67.

Wright (USA) as vice chairs and John Goormaghtigh as secretary. The most important decision of the conference was the approval of a constitution for the new body. It was provided that this would come into effect, and the new International Political Science Association would be born, as soon as four national associations had agreed to become collective members. The conference also drew up an ambitious programme of work for the new association and a 12-member provisional executive committee was appointed. The committee in turn elected Quincy Wright as its chair, with Marcel Bridel and Denis Brogan (UK) as vice-chairs and François Goguel as executive secretary and treasurer.[7] The association itself came into legal existence later in the same year when four national associations affiliated as collective members: those of Canada, France, India and the United States.[8]

In reviewing IPSA's subsequent history, the complexity of developments makes it more appropriate to adopt a thematic than a chronological approach. The obvious starting point is the constitution itself, and this provides us with a useful framework for an examination of other aspects of IPSA's institutional development.

*The constitution*

The constitution of the new International Political Science Association resembled in structure and content the constitutions of the other international scholarly federations that appeared at approximately the same time. It consisted of 36 articles grouped into 10 sections. These were as follows:

1. Name and headquarters (arts 1-4)
2. Objectives (art. 5)
3. Membership (arts 6-10)
4. The council (arts 11-19)
5. The executive committee (arts 20-26)
6. Finance (arts 27-30)
7. Dissolution (arts 31-32)
8. Amendments (art. 33)
9. Entry into force (art. 34)
10. Transitional provisions (arts 35-36)

---

[7] "International Political Science Association: summary report of the constituent conference held at Unesco House, 12-16 September 1949", *International social science bulletin* 1 (3/4) 1949, pp. 81-5.

[8] Ibid, p. 82.

Since 1949, the constitution has been amended on eight occasions. On all but one of these occasions the amendments were minor. The first two sets (in 1955 and 1958) were largely house-keeping ones, dealing with the composition of the council (notably, the introduction of alternate members) and of the executive committee (including precision of its size, the ex officio membership of the past president and provision for the succession of the first vice president in the event of a vacancy) and more explicit allocation of budgetary responsibility to the executive committee. In 1964 the constitution was further changed, to allow the executive committee rather than the council to elect the vice presidents. In 1970 the major changes were an increase in the size of the executive committee (from a minimum of 10 to 12, and from a maximum of 15 to 18) and a provision that it should meet annually; there were also minor changes in provisions for the agenda of council meetings and for delegation of responsibility within the executive. The single change in 1979 was more substantial: following the deliberations of a subcommittee chaired by Jean Laponce, the number of individual members that might be appointed to the council was reduced and the categories from which they were to be drawn were explicitly defined (in practice, the paradoxical effect of the amendment was to increase the number of individual members on the council, not to reduce it; see p. 23). In 1982, again, there was a single change, designed to recognise the formal appointment of a programme chair.

With the exception of these changes, the IPSA constitution continued up to the beginning of the 1990s substantially as it had been since 1949. By this time, only eight of its articles had been amended, and the changes were in most cases very small.[9] But it had also become clear that a constitution drafted in the 1940s needed a serious overhaul to take account of the very different realities of academic organisation in the 1990s. The issue was considered by a subcommittee of the executive committee chaired by Carole Pateman, and the recommendations of the subcommittee were approved by the council in 1991.

The changes of 1991 were designed to achieve a number of objectives: to render the language of the constitution more gender-neutral and more legally precise; to abolish redundant provisions; and to ensure that the constitution would reflect practices that had developed over the years. Major changes thus included the abolition of all references to the posts of executive secretary and treasurer (in practice, these had been combined since the very beginning, and the officer in question was known as the secretary

---

[9] Articles that had been amended by 1991 were 11, 13, 17, 20, 22, 24, 25 and 27.

general); provision was made for a quorum at council meetings; the post of honorary president was abolished (none had ever been appointed); provision was made for the formal audit of the association's accounts (rather than for inspection by three members of the council); and the two last sections (dealing with the entry of the constitution into force, and making transitional provision) were dropped.

In addition to the substantive amendment of articles that had already been amended and minor verbal changes in many more, the large-scale constitutional overhaul of 1991 affected an additional seven articles.[10] The final set of amendments, in 1997, made little additional change: the main substantive amendment permitted the number of individual members of the council to be increased, while a minor change was made in the definition of the responsibilities of the council.[11] Nevertheless, it is a striking tribute to the durability of the original constitution that 50 years after its birth most of its original articles (18) remain intact.[12]

In the rest of this chapter we consider certain of the structures of IPSA that are covered by major sections of the constitution—specifically, the council, the executive committee and IPSA's finances. Another major section, membership, is sufficiently important to be made the subject of a separate chapter (chapter 3). This leaves us with the six remaining sections of the constitution, which we comment on here.

The first section of the constitution, dealing with the association's name and headquarters, is a standard component in the constitutions of scholarly societies—especially international ones. The association was established under French law, a circumstance that has continuing significance, in that IPSA is still required to inform the French authorities of any changes in its constitution and in the composition of its executive committee, and does so regularly. This section of the constitution also provide that the headquarters of the association would be in Paris; Geneva and Brussels (other cities in which international associations have commonly located themselves) had also been considered, but proximity to Unesco, the precedent set by other international unions establishing themselves in Paris and the attractiveness of the city in terms of transport and available infra-

---

[10] In terms of substantive changes, articles 11, 13, 20 and 24 were amended once again; articles 2, 5, 10, 18, 26, 28 and 29 were amended for the first time; and articles 34, 35 and 36 were dropped.

[11] Apart from minor verbal changes, the articles affected were 11 (amended now for the fourth time!) and 15.

[12] The articles that have survived unchanged are 1, 2, 4, 6, 8, 9, 14-17, 21, 23 and 30-33.

structural support clinched the case for the capital of France.[13] This provision survived until 1991, when it was replaced by a provision that IPSA would be "legally registered" in Paris, but its secretariat would be at the same location as its secretary general. In actual fact, the IPSA secretariat has been gone from Paris since 1955, apart from the period 1960-67 when it returned there during Serge Hurtig's tenure as secretary general.

The second section, dealing with IPSA's objectives, is also a standard part of the constitution of any scholarly body. IPSA's general purpose was initially defined in article 5 as follows:

... to promote the advancement of political science throughout the world, by such means as:

(a) encouraging the establishment and development of national political science associations;

(b) facilitating the spread of information about significant developments in political science;

(c) organising conferences and round table discussions and providing other opportunities for personal contacts among political scientists;

(d) providing documentary and reference services and other forms of assistance to members; and

(e) promoting internationally planned research.

The significance of these objectives changed greatly over time. In the early years, much effort was devoted to encouraging the establishment of national associations in countries where none existed. Although this remains an objective of IPSA, the reality now is that in most countries where the scholarly community is sufficiently large to sustain a political science association, one exists. IPSA's response to the second and fourth objectives is most obvious in its publication programme, discussed in chapter 6; indeed, the wording of this point was amended in 1991 to refer to the publication of books, journals and a newsletter. The fifth objective has been realised mainly through IPSA's network of research committees and study groups (see chapter 5). But it is in the organisation of conferences and round tables that IPSA has arguably been most active over the years, and the third objective was amended in 1991 to draw attention to the centrality of the world congress in IPSA's affairs (see chapter 4).

The last four sections of the constitution were a necessary part of a document of this kind. Those dealing with dissolution of the association and with constitutional amendment have never been amended, and follow common practice in organisations such as IPSA. Dissolution of the associa-

---

[13] "Constituent conference" (1949), pp. 82-3.

tion may be declared by a two thirds majority of the council, in which case the association's assets pass to an international organisation with similar objectives, or are to be used for purposes compatible with IPSA's objectives (this is a standard provision in bodies recognised as having "charitable" status, and typically has implications for the taxable status of the association in the country in which it is located). The constitution itself may be amended by a two third majority. The last two sections (providing for the coming into force of the constitution and for the appointment of a provisional executive) were clearly of transitional significance only, yet, remarkably, they were dropped from the constitution only in 1991.

We may turn, then, to the structural evolution of IPSA, considering in turn its major organs: the council (including a discussion of the presidency), the executive committee and its subcommittees, and the secretariat, concluding with a brief account of how these are funded as part of an overview of IPSA's finances.

## The council

The legitimacy of IPSA derived initially from the reputations of the prominent political scientists invited by the Unesco director general to the constitutive meeting in Paris in 1949. Once the constitution came into effect, supreme authority passed to the council, which first met in 1952 in the Hague. The council is the body that corresponds to what other international scholarly associations refer to as the general assembly: it is the representative organ of the association's members.[14] Like other such bodies, IPSA responded to diversity of membership types by identifying one primary category of member – the collective member (this corresponded in effect to national political science associations). Unlike other such bodies, which typically relegate other categories of members to a status in which they are not represented, IPSA made an effort to ensure that individual members would be represented on its council.

The council has thus from the outset consisted of two categories of members: representatives of collective members, and individual members from countries or regions where there was no collective member. Such individual members were to be appointed by the executive committee. The number of representatives of collective members ranged from one in the

---

[14] The body is normally described in other comparable organisations as the "general assembly"; only the International Association of Legal Science and the International Economic Association join IPSA in using the designation "council"; and the International Sociological Association has an "assembly of councils".

case of smaller associations to three in the case of larger ones; in addition, the constitution was amended in the late 1950s to permit the designation of alternate members of the council to replace full members should they be unable to attend. In the early years, there was a provision that the number of individual members should not exceed the total number of representatives of collective members — a rather unnecessary provision in practice, since the number of individual members appointed was always small, even though the constitution was interpreted liberally in terms of eligibility for membership.

The constitution was amended in 1979, as we have seen, to restrict the number of individual members to a size not exceeding 25% of the total number of representatives of collective members. It was also provided that these would be appointed by the president, with the approval of the executive committee, from three categories: individual and associate members of IPSA from countries or regions where there is no collective member, chairs and secretaries of IPSA research committees and study groups, and boards of editors of IPSA publications. This reform was intended to make room for the appointment of representatives of research committees and study groups, and it indeed led to a much more active presence on the council of persons not necessarily connected to national associations. From 1979 to 1991 the president was required to consult the relevant national associations before appointing representatives of research committees, study groups and editorial board members to the council. In 1997 the constitution was again amended — once more as a consequence of pressure from research committees — to allow the proportion of individual members to be increased from 25% to 30% of the proportion of representatives of collective members.

The council is required to meet in regular session at least once every three years at a time and place designated by the executive committee. Not surprisingly, the executive committee sets the meeting to coincide with the triennial world congress. There is also a provision for a special session of the council, to be convened by the secretary general on the requisition of two thirds of the collective members of the association, but this provision has never been invoked.

The main function of the council is to oversee the long-term activities of the association. Of course, between congresses it necessarily delegates this power to the executive committee; indeed, one of the council's major functions is to elect this executive committee and the IPSA president. Originally, the council also elected IPSA's vice presidents, but in 1964 this right was transferred to the executive committee.

In addition to laying down guidelines for the future, the council considers all aspects of IPSA's affairs over the previous three years; the most general summary of these is typically found in the secretary general's report. Provision was made for receipt of reports from national associations until 1991, and from 1970 to 1991 there was provision for a prospective review by the president (in practice, the president continued to present a report even after this date). Other items can be placed on the council's agenda by the executive committee or by collective members. The council has particular powers in the area of financial control: it reviews the association's three-yearly financial reports (up to 1991 by the appointment of a three-person committee; after that, by considering an audited report). It reviews the association's financial prospects for the next triennial period and, indeed, up to 1997 it was required to approve the association's budget for this period (though in practice it had not been doing so). The council alone, of course, can amend the constitution, and it has done so on eight occasions, as we have seen. The council was originally also given two additional powers that it never used in the first 50 years of its existence: to appoint honorary presidents (a power abolished in 1991) and to adopt its own rules of procedure (a matter being considered for the first time in 2000).

The 16 occasions on which the council met are listed in table 2.1 (to this has been added also the constitutive meeting of the association in 1949, when IPSA's constitution was adopted). It will be noted that the first meeting outside Europe took place only in 1973, but since then there has been a good deal of circulation between continents (this is discussed later in connection with the world congress; see chapter 4).

In terms of its composition, it is clear that the early dominance of national associations continued for a long time. Notwithstanding the constitutional provision in the early decades that up to half of the membership of the council could be made up of individual members, in practice the executive committee appointed very few; certainly, the number never approached the number of representatives of collective members (see appendix 1 for a full list of council members).

A theme that will recur when we consider other aspects of IPSA's activities also emerges from analysis of the council's changing composition. This is the high visibility of European representation. The position is summarised in table 2.2, which groups council members by continent over three time periods: the first six regular meetings, 1952-67, the next five, 1970-82, and the most recent five, 1985-97. Although the proportion of west European representatives had declined to 36.9% by the most recent

| Table 2.1: Council meetings, 1949-97 | | | |
|---|---|---|---|
| No. | year | date | venue | members |
| 1. | 1949 | Sep 12-16 | Paris | 23 |
| 2. | 1952 | Sep 8-9 | Hague | 33 (7) |
| 3. | 1955 | Aug 19-20 | Stockholm | 35 (7) |
| 4. | 1958 | Sep 15 | Rome | 41 (3) |
| 5. | 1961 | Sep 25 | Paris | 41 (1) |
| 6. | 1964 | Sep 20 | Geneva | 41 (0) |
| 7. | 1967 | Sep 17 | Brussels | 43 (2) |
| 8. | 1970 | Aug 30 | Munich | 53 (3) |
| 9. | 1973 | Aug 19 | Montreal | 52 (3) |
| 10. | 1976 | Aug 16 | Edinburgh | 56 (4) |
| 11. | 1979 | Aug 12 | Moscow | 63 (5) |
| 12. | 1982 | Aug 8 | Rio de Janeiro | 75 (11) |
| 13. | 1985 | Jul 15 | Paris | 71 (17) |
| 14. | 1988 | Aug 28 | Washington | 75 (12) |
| 15. | 1991 | Jul 22 | Buenos Aires | 72 (14) |
| 16. | 1994 | Aug 21 | Berlin | 74 (14) |
| 17. | 1997 | Aug 17 | Seoul | 66 (13) |

Note: the first meeting was officially designated an "international political science conference"; the first formal council meeting was the one here numbered 2. The number in brackets after the number of members of the council refers to the number of individual members; the others were representatives of collective members of IPSA.

period, it was still high—a function in part of the relatively high level of development of the discipline in Europe, but also of that continent's politically fragmented status.

The pattern of women's representation on the council is relatively predictable. Although it has not been possible to infer the gender of all members from their names, it is clear that women have historically constituted a rather small minority (9%). However, if we look at the pattern over time, using the three periods of table 2.2, an increase is obvious. During the first period, the proportion of women was 2% (accounted for mainly by Lolo Krusius-Ahrenberg, who represented Finland in the first three councils). This increased to only 4% in the intermediate period, and for the 1985-97 period the proportion of women was 16%.

| Table 2.2: Council members by continent, 1952-97 | | | | | | | |
|---|---|---|---|---|---|---|---|
| Continent | 1952-67 | | 1970-82 | | 1985-97 | | total |
| | no. | % | no. | % | no. | % | no. | % |
| Africa | 2 | 0.9 | 10 | 3.3 | 14 | 3.9 | 26 | 2.9 |
| America, North | 31 | 13.2 | 41 | 13.7 | 55 | 15.4 | 127 | 14.3 |
| America, South | 10 | 4.3 | 18 | 6.0 | 21 | 5.9 | 49 | 5.5 |
| Asia | 26 | 16.1 | 48 | 16.0 | 60 | 16.8 | 134 | 15.0 |
| Europe, East, etc | 32 | 13.7 | 58 | 19.4 | 64 | 17.9 | 154 | 17.3 |
| Europe, West | 128 | 54.7 | 118 | 39.5 | 132 | 36.9 | 378 | 42.4 |
| Oceania | 5 | 2.1 | 6 | 2.0 | 12 | 3.4 | 23 | 2.6 |
| total | 234 | 100.0 | 299 | 100.0 | 358 | 100.0 | 891 | 100.0 |

As already mentioned, one of the most important functions of the IPSA council is the election of the IPSA president. Following the work of the preparatory committee presided over by Walter Sharp in 1948-49, Raymond Aron chaired the constitutive meeting of IPSA in 1949 at which Quincy Wright was designated president. When the first meeting of the council formed under the constitution took place in 1952, the regular procedures for presidential elections commenced. It should also be noted that, in view of the symbolic and substantive importance of the office and the need to maximise time for reflection on potential candidates, the constitution was amended in 1970 to require the executive committee itself to designate a presidential candidate or candidates one year in advance of the formal election (one of the few contested presidential elections had taken place in the council in 1967). Because of the influence of the executive within any organisation, the reality is that the most intense debates regarding presidential succession now take place within the executive committee rather than on the floor of the council.

The list of presidents of IPSA is reported in table 2.3. Once again, the dominance of western scholars is clear. It was only in 1979 that the first political scientist from outside Europe and North America was elected (Candido Mendes from Brazil). The election of Kinhide Mushakoji of Japan in 1985 marked the first occasion on which an Asian scholar assumed the post, and it is clear that, largely because of global developments within the discipline, the presidency is now much more open to all regions.

One geopolitical issue that was tackled rather obliquely was that of the division between the west and the communist world. Although the council considered the election of an East European president on a number of oc-

| Table 2.3: IPSA presidents, 1949-99 | | |
| --- | --- | --- |
| Quincy Wright | University of Chicago | 1949-52 |
| William A Robson | London School of Economics | 1952-55 |
| James K Pollock | University of Michigan | 1955-58 |
| Jacques Chapsal | FNSP/IEP, Paris | 1958-61 |
| D N Chester | Nuffield College, Oxford | 1961-64 |
| Jacques Freymond | IUHEI, Geneva | 1964-67 |
| Carl J Friedrich | Harvard University | 1967-70 |
| Stein Rokkan | University of Bergen | 1970-73 |
| Jean Laponce | University of British Columbia | 1973-76 |
| Karl Deutsch | Harvard University | 1976-79 |
| Candido Mendes | SBI, Rio de Janeiro | 1979-82 |
| Klaus von Beyme | University of Heidelberg | 1982-85 |
| Kinhide Mushakoji | UN University, Tokyo | 1985-88 |
| Guillermo O'Donnell | CEBRAP, São Paulo/Notre Dame | 1988-91 |
| Carole Pateman | UCLA, Los Angeles | 1991-94 |
| Jean Leca | FNSP/IEP, Paris | 1994-97 |
| Theodore J Lowi | Cornell University | 1997-00 |

casions between 1967 and 1982, with Poland supplying the most obvious candidates, it stopped short of so significant a gesture.[15] However, the post of "first vice president" provided a useful mechanism for maintaining inter-bloc balance: during the period 1979-85, for instance, the post was held by a Soviet scholar, Georgii Shakhnazarov, as recognition of the significance of the communist bloc, and this arrangement seems to have played a significant role in preventing the kind of inter-bloc divisions that were to ravage other international federations. Since then, the post of first vice president has become essentially one of primacy among the other vice presidents (see appendix 2 for a list of first vice presidents and vice presidents).

## The executive committee

A temporary executive committee of the new International Political Science Association met for the first time in Zurich (Switzerland) on 4-9 September 1950. When the constitution came into force later in the same year, the regular executive committee took over. In terms of provisions for its

---

[15] See Stanislaw Ehrlich, "IPSA's lining and kitchen: some very personal remarks", *Participation* 19 (3) 1995, pp. 7-12.

composition and structure, it is "normal" in the context of comparable international bodies. A list of members of the executive committee is given in appendix 2, and a list of meetings in appendix 3.

The executive committee originally consisted of a minimum of 10 and a maximum of 15 members elected by the council for a three-year period (these figures included the president and vice presidents). The constitution was changed in the late 1950s to permit the outgoing president to serve as an ex-officio member of the executive committee and to allow alternate members of the council and the outgoing secretary general to stand for election (the outgoing secretary general's right to stand was abolished in 1991). The minimum and maximum limits on executive size were increased in 1970, to 12 and 18 respectively. It is a striking feature of IPSA – as, indeed, of other bodies that permit this flexibility in the size of their executive committees – that the upper limit quickly comes to be seen as the norm rather than as a boundary. Thus, the size of the executive committee rose from 11 in 1950 to 13 in 1952 and its maximum size of 15 in 1955; it remained at this level until the maximum was increased in 1970, after which it has always consisted of 18 members.

The executive committee is responsible, in between congresses, for the implementation of IPSA's programme: for organising congresses and other academic activities, overseeing the association's publications, monitoring the work of research committees and study groups, and managing the financial and other affairs of the association. In effect, the executive committee is the linchpin of IPSA. Its meetings are chaired by the IPSA president, and are attended normally by the editors of IPSA publications. Since the 1950s, the constitution has permitted alternates designated by national associations to replace absent members of the executive committee at meetings of the committee, but this power has rarely been used.

Given the importance of the executive committee, it will be useful to consider some of the principles that have guided its first 50 years of activity. The founders of the association recognised from the outset that political science, as a discipline, had some peculiarities. On the whole, it was not very well known, and was even disliked by certain political authorities. As a scientific discipline, it struggled with the kinds of impediments arising from academic underdevelopment and lack of definition of its identity that have been described in chapter 1. Furthermore, political science has not been understood in the same way by all countries and cultures, and barely maintains an existence in many countries. How then could it be made into an international discipline? A number of principles that the executive committee has followed may be identified.

The first principle can be nicknamed the "diplomatic brotherhood" for the advancement of the discipline. This was especially important before the fall of communism, and meant that, in order to further the development of political science in the world, the members of the executive committee would seek to promote friendship to overcome the distrust that kept their countries apart in everyday politics. This was especially important during the period of the cold war. The holding of the 1979 congress in Moscow is an example of the fruits of this cooperation: it took place despite the opposition, mobilised in varying degrees, of two very different groups: the secret services of certain countries, and human rights groups in these and other countries. There is, however, evidence that the Moscow congress had a very considerable impact on the legitimacy of the discipline in communist-controlled countries, as we have seen.[16]

A second principle is that of tolerance. In practice, tolerance means a balance between the demands of internationalism and the requirements of the discipline. Indeed, the association is perpetually caught in the crossfire of the requirements of participation and representation based on criteria of appropriate geographical representation (including regions, ethnic groups and political regimes) on the one hand and, on the other hand, based on scholarly excellence (but recognising a diversity of methodological approaches). Since there are several definitions of both the groups that are to be represented (including women and younger scholars) and the components of excellence in political science, the potential for conflict between societies where the discipline is very developed and others where political science is only beginning to develop (and, indeed, within the former group) has always been considerable. In this context, the principle of tolerance acquires an exceptional significance.

The history of the IPSA executive committee illustrates the balance between regions, nationalities, ideologies and disciplinary approaches that mark out the pluralism of the association. To date, 146 noted individuals have sat on the executive committee . They are broken down by continent in table 2.4. This shows that, while western Europe has been very strongly represented, its dominance has been diminishing in the past 25 years, with a growth especially in African and Asian representation. The number of women members has been very small. It is interesting to note too that the tendency in the past for members of the executive to serve for more than two terms has ended; in recent years, the only member to serve a third term has been the president, who has typically served on the executive

---

[16]Máté Szabó, "Political science in Hungary", *Participation* 22 (2) 1998, pp. 4-6.

| Table 2.4: Executive committee members by continent, 1949-99 | | | |
|---|---|---|---|
| Continent | 1949-75 | 1976-99 | Total |
| Africa | 1 | 6 | 7 |
| America, North | 11 | 9 | 20 |
| America, South | 5 | 5 | 10 |
| Asia | 12 | 16 | 28 |
| Europe, East | 12 | 9 | 21 |
| Europe, West | 32 | 28 | 60 |
| Total | 73 | 73 | 146 |

committee for two terms before becoming president. Of the 146 members, 61 have served for one term only, 61 for two terms, 11 for three terms, 10 for four terms, two for five terms and one for six. It should be noted that IPSA is unusual among international scholarly unions in that its constitution does not prohibit executive committee members from serving a third term; but the unwritten rule now is that all executive committee members stand down after two terms unless they succeed to the presidency.

Women were slow to gain entry to the executive committee. In all, only 10 out of 146 executive committee members have been women. The first woman to be elected was Sirkka Sinkkonen of Finland, in 1973. She was followed after a long gap by Inge Perko-Separovic of Yugoslavia in 1982. Carole Pateman of Australia (later to become IPSA's first woman president) and Elisa Reis of Brazil followed in 1988, and six others were elected later.

### Subcommittees

In its early years, IPSA established a number of subcommittees in such areas as "round tables, seminars and congresses", "the development of political science" and "research programme", as well as on "constitution and electoral procedure". Many other once-off subcommittees were appointed subsequently, to consider a wide range of academic, administrative and financial matters.

The first standing subcommittee was the *programme committee*, created in 1958 in Rome to plan the academic programme of the world congress. Initially entirely a small subcommittee of the executive committee, it acted in many respects as an executive within the executive, reflecting the centrality of the world congress in IPSA's affairs at that time. In its early years,

| Table 2.5: Programme chairs, 1976-00 | | |
|---|---|---|
| Richard L Merritt | USA | 1976-79 |
| Guillermo O'Donnell | Argentina | 1979-82 |
| Francesco Kjellberg | Oslo | 1982-85 |
| Harold Jacobson | USA | 1985-88 |
| Jean Leca | France | 1988-91 |
| Robert Goodin | Australia | 1991-94 |
| I William Zartman | USA | 1994-97 |
| William M Lafferty | Norway | 1997-00 |

the committee was chaired by the IPSA president but in 1976 the practice of appointing a separate programme chair was initiated (see table 2.5 for a list of chairs). In 1982 the constitution was changed to institutionalise the standing of the programme committee and to make provision for the appointment of a programme chair (by this stage, this amounted to the formalisation of an established practice). By the 1980s, the programme committee consisted typically of the president, the secretary general and the vice presidents (a formula that tended to result in a regional balance), together with external members representing a range of subfields.

Disciplinary development was also the principal factor behind the creation of a second subcommittee, the *committee on research committees and study groups*. In the course of the 1970s and the 1980s the number of research committees and study groups more than doubled, increasing from 21 to 43; by the end of the 1990s it had reached 50 (see chapter 5). It quickly became clear that, notwithstanding the high level of productivity of many groups, a more rigorous set of procedures was needed to manage the processes of recognition of new groups and monitoring of the activities of existing ones if the association were to maintain its credibility and legitimacy as sponsor of cutting-edge research. In 1979 the executive committee decided to establish a monitoring subcommittee was established, with Daniel Frei as chair. The terms of reference of the committee required it to make recommendations to the executive committee on the recognition of new research committees and study groups, on changes in status of committees and groups or on the possible withdrawal of recognition, and on related matters. With a view to avoiding the ugly expression "committee on ... committee", the "committee" was renamed "commission" in 1982. This body has been responsible for ensuring that the conduct of the affairs of recognised research committees and study groups is compatible with universal principles of scholarship, that membership is appropriately open and that various regions and approaches are represented. All research committees and study groups are required to submit regular reports to the commission (see table 2.6 for a list of chairs).

A third standing subcommittee of the executive committee, the *committee on long-term planning*, was created in 1979 and operated under the vigorous leadership of its first chair, Kinhide Mushakoji. Its mandate was to advise the executive committee on longer-term planning issues and to recommend on new initiatives designed to further IPSA's mission. It presented regular reports to the executive committee, and considered additional matters referred to it by the executive committee. It was chaired by Inge Perko-Separovic for a period (1985-88), before being taken over again by Kinhide Mushakoji. In 1989, however, it was absorbed by a committee on global environmental change, whose long-term spin-off was the creation of a study group (now a research committee) in this area.

IPSA's concern to maximise participation of young scholars was reflected in the creation of a prize for the best paper by a young scholar, and by the establishment in 1988 of a *committee on awards* which was specifically asked to recommend mechanisms for increasing the participation of young scholars. Later renamed the committee on young scholars and awards, it was chaired in succession by Itzhak Galnoor (1988-91), Pierre Allan (1991-94) and Takeshi Sasaki (1994-97).

In 1989 the executive committee established a fifth standing subcommittee. This followed receipt of a report on the status of women in IPSA prepared by Carole Pateman, and the new subcommittee, entitled the *committee on women's issues*, was chaired initially by Carole Pateman. Its objectives were to monitor the position of women in IPSA and recommend on ways in which action could be taken to improve this. Its second chair was Maureen Covell (1991-97).

| Table 2.6: Chairs, Commission on research committees and study groups, 1980-00 | | |
| --- | --- | --- |
| Daniel Frei | Switzerland | 1979-82 |
| Dieter Senghaas | Germany | 1982-85 |
| Olof Ruin | Sweden | 1985-88 |
| Kenneth Newton | UK | 1988-91 |
| Pippa Norris | UK | 1991-94 |
| Hans-Dieter Klingemann | Germany | 1994-97 |
| Ursula Vogel | UK | 1997-00 |

The standing committee structure was entirely overhauled in February 1998, when the following set of standing subcommittees was established:

- *Committee on organisation and procedure*: a new committee, chaired by Dalchoong Kim

- *Committee on the congress programme*: a continuation of the former programme committee, but with broadened terms of reference, chaired by William M Lafferty

- *Committee on research and training*: a continuation of the former commission on research committees, but with greatly extended terms of reference, chaired by Ursula Vogel

- *Committee on awards*: a continuation of the existing committee, but with a broader mandate, chaired by Helen Shestopal

- *Committee on the status of women and diversity of participation* (to be known in abbreviated form as the *committee on participation*): a continuation of the former committee on women scholars, but with extended terms of reference, chaired by Renato Boschi.

In addition to these, the executive committee has created a range of other subcommittees at different times in the past. The longest standing of these was the visa committee, an essential body at a time when travel was subject to many formal restrictions. In addition, a number of ad-hoc subcommittees, or subcommittees appointed to examine and report on a single issue, have been created. These include subcommittees on various aspects of the constitution; on various aspects of finance; on diversification; on the admission of collective members; on the representation of collective members on the IPSA council; on language policy; on travelling workshops; on the human dimension to global change; on the IPSA book series; and on other aspects of IPSA publications. In addition, of course, the executive committee has appointed a range of search committees to recommend appointments in such areas as the post of secretary general and the editors of IPSA's publications.

*The secretariat*

The day-to-day affairs of the association are administered by the secretary general, with the help of an administrator and possibly additional short-term staff. The running costs of the secretariat are covered by a budget approved by the executive committee. Although the post of secretary general has been so designated informally for many decades, it is of some interest that it was written into the constitution only in 1991. Prior to that, the person known as secretary general was simply the individual who combined two posts defined in the constitution from the beginning: that of executive secretary, and that of treasurer (the constitution specifically permitted the merger of these two posts). The executive secretary and treasurer (and, later, the secretary general) were to be appointed by the executive committee rather than being elected by the council.

The original IPSA constitution required the executive secretary to fill a number of predictable roles. He or she was to prepare a report on the work of the association between meetings of the council, to make arrangements for meetings of the council as appropriate, to convene meetings of the executive committee and to make the necessary arrangements for them, and to appoint additional administrative staff as appropriate. The treasurer was to prepare three-yearly accounts for the council and to supervise the receipt, disbursement and custody of moneys on behalf of the association. The 1991 amendment of the constitution, designed to reflect the merger of the two posts in practice since 1949, formally transferred the existing responsibilities of the executive secretary and of the treasurer to the secretary general, who was also allocated additional tasks (again, reflecting what had become practice): to supervise the archives of the association and to publish a newsletter. In 1979 there was a brief experiment with the appointment of an associate secretary general, but this was discontinued after a short time.

The secretary general attends all the executive committee meetings but is not a member of the committee. Since the secretary general is normally a full-time academic who can devote only part of his or her time to managing IPSA's affairs, much day-to-day responsibility has passed into the hands of a full-time administrator. The first full-time administrator was Michèle David (France, 1962-67), and she was followed by Michèle Scohy (Belgium, 1967-76), Liette Boucher (Canada, 1976-88), Lise Fog (Norway, 1988-94), Louise Delaney (Ireland, 1994-98) and Margaret Brindley (1998-00).

The secretariat has been located in different parts of the world, according to the country of residence of the secretary general, who is nominated by the executive committee for a renewable three-year term. Thus, the secretariat has been located at the Fondation Nationale des Sciences Politiques in Paris (1949-55, 1961-67), the Carnegie Endowment in Brussels (1955-60), the Institut de Sociologie of the Université Libre de Bruxelles (1967-76), the University of Ottawa (1976-1988), the University of Oslo (1988-94) and University College Dublin (1994-2000); see table 2.7 for a list of secretaries general. Although it is of little administrative significance, the Fondation

| Table 2.7: IPSA secretaries general, 1949-99 | | |
|---|---|---|
| François Goguel | FNSP, Paris | 1949-50 |
| Jean Meynaud | FNSP, Paris | 1950-55 |
| John Goormaghtigh | Carnegie Endowment, Brussels | 1955-60 |
| Serge Hurtig | FNSP, Paris | 1960-67 |
| André Philippart | Université Libre de Bruxelles | 1967-76 |
| John Trent | University of Ottawa | 1976-88 |
| Francesco Kjellberg | University of Oslo | 1988-94 |
| John Coakley | University College Dublin | 1994-00 |

Nationale des Sciences Politiques in Paris continues to be the legal head-quarters of the association.

In addition to the association's correspondence, the secretary general is responsible for the management of funds, the administration of the three categories of members (collective, individual and associate), the publication of the association's newsletter, *Participation,* and other documents, as well as the organisation of the working meetings of the executive committee and the preparation of round table meetings and congresses. In the late 1990s, maintenance of the association's web page has been added to these responsibilities. In practical terms, for the most part, the preparation of a round table meeting is handed over to the association members most closely involved with the host institution, whereas the preparation of a congress falls within the realm of the national political science association of the country where it is to be held and immediate administrative responsibilities tend to be devolved to a local organising committee.

As in most large organisations, the secretary general's role extends beyond administrative tasks. In order for an organisation to function properly, the secretary general must work closely with the president, the executive committee and its subcommittees, and he or she should be able to act as some kind of institutional memory for the association. Over time, indeed, as the activities in which the association is involved have become more numerous and more complex, the burdens of the office have accumulated; nevertheless, after its first 50 years IPSA continues to adhere to the model of the part-time secretary general rather than adopting the path of many other international scholarly bodies whose affairs are managed by a full-time executive director.

*Finance*

Finally, we need to consider the important issue of the material infra-structure of the association, of which the most central aspect is finance. IPSA's constitution originally specified four sources of revenue for the association: annual dues levied on collective members at a rate determined by the council itself; membership subscriptions of individual and associate members; net proceeds from sales of publications; and subventions from public institutions and fees for special services. For most of IPSA's history, its income came predominantly from two sources: grants and membership dues.

In the early years, IPSA depended heavily on support from international bodies, of which the most important by far was Unesco. IPSA's particularly strong relationship with Unesco was unsurprising, since, after all, the latter had sponsored IPSA's very foundation in 1949. Unesco made an initial grant of $5,750 to assist with infrastructural development and organisational costs. This grant was renewed annually, and had increased to $7,500 by 1954 and to $10,000 by 1967. It had exceeded $20,000 by the mid-1980s. It then stabilised, in each of the years 1991 to 1995, at exactly $18,389. Following the establishment of the International Social Science Council (ISSC) in 1952, this grant was transmitted to IPSA through the ISSC, of which IPSA had become a constitutive member association. In addition, and especially in the early years, Unesco made generous grants for other purposes, of which the most important was IPSA's triennial congress.

The formal relationship between IPSA and the ISSC/Unesco changed after 1995, the last year in which the annual block grant from Unesco to member associations of the ISSC was made. Following policy changes originating in the Unesco general assembly, the basis of the award to ISSC member associations changed fundamentally in 1996. For each subsequent biennium (1996-97, 1998-99 and 2000-01) member associations were invited to tender for contracts for specific academic projects. In practice, IPSA has been relatively successful in this process, and has managed to maintain its share of ISSC funding.

Although revenue from grants of this kind accounted for the great bulk of IPSA's income in the 1950s and the 1960s, the association's steadiest and most predictable source has for long been membership dues. This depended on two factors: IPSA's success in recruiting members, and the level at which subscription rates were pegged. While the significance of this source has varied greatly from year to year, it would not be inaccurate to say that membership revenue accounted for approximately 10-20 per cent of the total in the 1950s, rising to 30-40 per cent by the 1990s.

Revenue from sales of publications was initially projected as an important source of income, but IPSA's limited publishing activity reduced its significance. Though circulating widely, the *International political science abstracts* were seen as a contribution to the academic community rather than a commercial activity, and initially generated little revenue for the association. But this essentially revenue neutral status in respect of publishing activities began to change in the last two decades of the twentieth century. IPSA started to receive a steady royalty from sales of books in its books series. The new *International political science review*, launched in 1980, built on its solid academic reputation by becoming also a commercial success, and a contract with a new publisher in 1994 resulted in a very significant increase in net income from sales. Finally, the *Abstracts* began to generate a sizeable surplus, and this increased steadily. In particular, the launch of the *Abstracts* in CD-rom form in 1995 provided a major boost, resulting in a very large increase in net revenue. By 1999, approximately 17 per cent of IPSA's revenue derived from royalties on its publications.

But IPSA's sound financial basis cannot be accounted for entirely by direct income. Special funds to organise round table discussions and congresses have come over the years from the generosity of national associations, universities, academies, social sciences funding agencies and other institutions that provide either money or services. The success of the scientific gatherings of IPSA can be attributed in large part to these different groups, whose assistance has been most pronounced at times of world congresses.

Combining the administrative meetings of the executive committee with the scientific organisation of the round table meetings and congresses has, then, allowed the association to operate at low cost. Over IPSA's lifespan, its finances have been greatly assisted by the fact that most members of the executive committee have been able to benefit from outside financial support. In many cases, this would not have been forthcoming for a purely administrative meeting, but IPSA has been careful to ensure that its business meetings normally coincide with major academic events. Furthermore, the host association or university has typically been in a favourable position to obtain grants which allowed it to underwrite in most cases the accommodation costs of the executive committee members.

The outcome, then, has tended to be a comfortable excess of revenue over expenditure, especially in recent years. An outline of IPSA's receipts and outgoings is given in appendix 4. This will show that, in addition to a predictably steady increase over the decades, both revenue and expenditure have tended to jump sharply in congress years and to drop back equally dramatically in post-congress years. Over all, it will be seen, the association has managed to remain in a healthy financial condition after its first 50 years of existence.

# 3 / MEMBERSHIP

The vigour of any international scholarly body—especially if it has the character of a federation—will depend critically on the quality and commitment of its members. The increase in the number of members of IPSA indeed demonstrates clearly the organisational progress of the discipline at international level during the past 50 years. Whereas there were just four national member associations of IPSA in 1949, there were 42 collective members by 1999. The number of associate members climbed steadily until 1969, when it exceeded 200; although it has declined since then for reasons to be discussed later, it still remains in the region of 100. The number of individual members has also climbed steadily, from an initial 52 in 1952. It peaked at more than 1,600 in 1985, and since then it has typically been comfortably in excess of 1,000. In the remainder of this chapter we consider the features of each type of membership.

IPSA's tripartite membership structure dates right from the association's foundation. The *collective member* is a national or regional association considered to be representative of political science in a given country or region. As a general rule, there is only one collective member per country or region. IPSA's policy is to encourage the formation of a common organisation or representative when two associations from the same country, equally representative of political science in that country, apply for collective member status. Each collective members is represented on the IPSA council. The *associate member* is an international or national association, organisation or institution which, in political science or in fields of endeavour similar to that of political science, pursues goals akin to those of the association. It may, at its own request, be represented at council meetings but without voting rights. Finally, an *individual member* is defined as anyone considered sufficiently qualified in the field of political science, either professionally or otherwise. Individual members are not required to be members of their national associations. A number of individual members are appointed to the council by the president following a specific procedure.

The benefits of membership vary from one category to another. The current position has changed only slightly from that pertaining in IPSA's early years, with developments arising from IPSA's new publishing ventures accounting for the largest changes. All types of member receive IPSA publications (the *International political science review* and *Participation*) and are given access both to information circulated by IPSA and to various forms of networking. For collective members, the most obvious additional benefit is the right to influence IPSA's policies through membership of the council, and the right of their representatives to be elected to the executive committee. Members of collective member associations may join IPSA research committees even if they are not individual members of IPSA. Associate members can receive additional publications (including the *International political science abstracts*, the *International social science journal* and the microfiche or CD editions of congress papers) at a reduced rate. Individual members have access to IPSA publications on the same basis as associate members, but in addition receive a very substantial reduction in IPSA congress registration fees; they, and they alone, may be officers of IPSA research committees.

### Collective members

IPSA was, as indicated already, created not only as a consequence of a Unesco initiative but also through the efforts and commitment of four national associations (those of France, Canada, the United States and India). Its constitutive conference sought not only to lay the structural foundations of IPSA but also to ensure its long-term survival by encouraging the creation of a range of national political science associations. It also tackled the question of fee structure for collective members.

Generally speaking, there appear to be three approaches to fee structure in international scholarly organisations that are made up wholly or in part of national member associations. The principles may be labelled those of equality, proportionality and categorisation. Organisations whose collective national membership fees are based on the principle of *equality* (i.e. each member association pays the same amount) are typically small ones with a minimal secretariat or central servicing body, and are thus capable of running on a relatively small budget.[1] In associations applying the principle of *proportionality*, each affiliated national group pays a fee that is directly related to some measure of wealth. This may be based either on na-

---

[1] Examples are the International Federation of Societies of Classical Studies, the International Economic History Association and the International Union of Prehistoric and Protohistoric Sciences (the last of which treats all members equally but, unusually, charges no fee at all!). This and the following remarks are based on an examination of the constitutions and procedural documents of a wide range of associations.

tional wealth or on the wealth of national associations themselves.[2] The third approach, *categorisation*, takes account of variations in capacity to pay and possibly other indicators, but it translates these into broad payment bands rather than seeking to relate them proportionately to fees payable. [3] Typically, but not universally, there is a relationship between fee payable and representation in the body's central organs.

If we look at the history of IPSA's approach to the fee structure of collective members, it appears to have fallen into three phases. In the first, dating from IPSA's very foundation, the dominant principle was proportionality. In 1967 IPSA moved to a form of categorisation, though in large measure this was an acknowledgement of a development that was already taking place in practice: apart from a couple of outliers, member associations had by this point been grouped into three categories. The third phase began in 1997, when the 1967 system was revisited and replaced by another categorisation based on slightly different principles.

Under the original system, each member association was expected to pay a fee equivalent to 1 per cent of its income from its own members, subject to a minimum fee of $10 and a maximum of $200.[4] It is also clear that from the outset associations were divided into three categories in terms of the number of members they returned to the council—one, two or three members.[5] The constitution leaves it to the executive committee to determine the actual number, subject to the proviso that no member may have more than three representatives; but at an early stage it was decided, naturally enough, to link this with the size and strength of the national political science community, and therefore, though indirectly and rather less precisely, with fee payable.

While the three-tiered representation system has survived with little change over the past 50 years, the fee structure has evolved considerably.

---

[2] Examples (though varying in the degree to which they strictly match this principle) are the International Institute of Administrative Sciences, the International Union of Anthropological and Ethnological Sciences and the International Sociological Association.

[3] Examples are the International Geographical Unit (with 15 categories), the International Mathematical Union (five categories) and the International Federation for Mental Health (four categories).

[4] "International Political Science Association: summary of the constituent conference held in Unesco House, 12-15 September 1949", *International social science bulletin* 1 (3/4), 1949, pp. 81-85.

[5] At the 1952 council meeting, for instance, Britain, France and the United States were entitled to three members each, Canada, India, Poland and Sweden to two, and all other countries (Austria, Belgium, Greece, Israel and Mexico) to one.

By 1967, collective members fell into a number of different payment categories, ranging from $21 to $1,000, which were not perfectly correlated to their council representation.[6] The 1967 council meeting sought to systematise this by introducing a formal categorisation scheme with effect from 1968. The lowest category was made up of countries contributing less than 1 per cent of the Unesco budget, who would now be required to pay a basic minimum of $100 a year; next were countries contributing between 1 and 2 per cent of the Unesco budget, who should pay $150 per year; in the third category were countries contributing between 2 and 10 per cent of the Unesco budget, who were assessed at $300 per year; and, finally, countries contributing a larger share of the Unesco budget were to pay in rough proportion to their Unesco shares. The last provision affected two countries: the USSR, which was assessed at $700, and the USA, assessed at $1,500. Associations finding difficulty with this scheme were invited to apply to the executive committee for temporary reductions in their contributions.

For three decades, this remained the basis of IPSA's collective member fee structure; although fees increased incrementally, the relative position of the various associations was broadly maintained. Efforts to change the 1967 system enjoyed varying degrees of success. At the Montreal council meeting in 1973, for instance, an effort was made to insulate IPSA against inflation by providing for a substantial annual increase in all collective member subscriptions for as long as the very high rate of inflation, the plague of the period for associations such as IPSA, continued. Further sharp increases were made in 1976, and wealthier associations were invited to make additional voluntary contributions. Given the uneven pace of economic development globally and the stability of the relative positions of the various associations established in 1967, significant anomalies developed over time. It became increasingly difficult to resolve these inconsistencies by mechanical means, but neither did it prove possible to adopt a new fee structure.

Instead, IPSA responded pragmatically to developments that had a bearing on the capacity of its members to pay. IPSA granted de facto recognition to the split in the Belgian association along linguistic lines in 1976, and since then two Belgian associations have paid and been represented separately. Similar but less drastic compromises have been adopted in

---

[6] Pakistan, $21; India, Israel and the Netherlands, $25; Australia, Austria, Brazil, Czechoslovakia, Denmark, Finland, FR Germany, Italy, Japan, Norway, Poland, Spain, Turkey and Yugoslavia $50; Sweden $80; Argentina, Belgium, Switzerland and the UK $100; France $140; USSR $150; and the USA $1,000.

other associations, though these may be substantially invisible even to IPSA. The break-up of Yugoslavia, the Soviet Union and Czechoslovakia resulted in reduced fees and council representation for the "rump" states in these three cases from 1992, 1994 and 1994, respectively. In 1994 the executive committee also agreed to a (retrospective) modified fee structure for former communist-governed states (to take account of the collapse in social science funding there), by which they would pay 33% of their "normal" fee for 1993, 50% for 1994, 67% for 1995 and 83% for 1996, rising to the full "normal" fee in 1997. Nevertheless, by 1997 the broad proportions established 30 years earlier survived: associations in the three largest categories now paid respectively $580, $885 and $1,775, while the United States was liable for $8,890 and the Soviet Union would have been liable for $2,750 (in fact, the successor to the Soviet association, the Russian Political Science Association, was charged a significantly reduced amount).

In 1997, IPSA entered a third phase in terms of its financial relationship with collective members. Once again, a form of categorisation was adopted, but this time the groups were linked to the average of two criteria (location on the revised United Nations table of payments, and number of members in the national association), and provision was made for periodic revision.[7] Collective members were grouped into five categories on the basis of these criteria, the categories corresponding respectively to one, two, four, six and sixteen units of payment (the value of a unit of payment was fixed in 1997 at $500). Provision was also made in respect of less wealthy countries for a fee amounting to half a unit of payment (or, in certain circumstances, to even less than this).

But payment of a membership fee has not been the only criterion for membership of the association. Indeed, IPSA has from the outset tried to ensure that associations admitted as collective members were organisationally sound and were representative of political science in their country. In other words, they had to be based on well established political science teaching and research programmes as well as on a sufficient number of qualified political scientists. Each application has been vetted to ensure its conformity with these conditions.

How, then, has the actual recruitment of collective members of IPSA proceeded? Thanks to the participation of several leading political scientists at the 1949 conference and the Hague congress (1952) on an individual basis, IPSA gained eight new national associations as members. Israel, Po-

---

[7] The switch from the Unesco to the United Nations system had no implications for relative weightings.

| Table 3.1: The first 20 collective members | |
|---|---|
| **The founder members:** | |
| American Political Science Association | 1949 |
| Association française de science politique | 1949 |
| Canadian Political Science Association | 1949 |
| Indian Political Science Association | 1949 |
| | |
| **The early members:** | |
| Israel Political Science Association | 1950 |
| Polish Association of Political Science | 1950 |
| Political Studies Association of the UK | 1950 |
| Swedish Political Science Association | 1950 |
| Austrian Political Science Association | 1951 |
| Institut belge de science politique | 1951 |
| Hellenic Political Science Association | 1951 |
| *Mexican Political Science Association* | *1951* |
| Brazilian Institute of Law and Political Science | 1952 |
| Finnish Political Science Association | 1952 |
| German Political Science Association | 1952 |
| Italian Political Science Association | 1952 |
| Japanese Association of Political Science | 1952 |
| Yugoslav Association of Political Science | 1952 |
| Australian Political Studies Association | 1953 |
| Dutch Political Science Association | 1953 |

land, the United Kingdom and Sweden were accepted as collective members in 1950, while Austria, Belgium, Greece and Mexico were accredited in 1951. A further eight national associations were given collective member status in 1952 and 1953. The newly admitted associations were from the Federal Republic of Germany, Finland, Italy, Yugoslavia, Japan and Brazil (1952), and from the Netherlands and Australia (1953).

Three further members joined in 1955 (Ceylon, Cuba and the Soviet Union), but following this boom the number of member countries increased only slowly. From 1955 to 1964, the number of collective members rose from 23 to 29. In fact, there had been a considerable influx of new members: Egypt and Norway (1956), Lebanon and Spain (1958), Switzerland and Denmark (1961), and Czechoslovakia, Pakistan and Turkey (1964). However, there were also losses: the Mexican and Cuban associations were disbanded (1957), and the membership of the Ceylonese association was terminated (1959). The membership of the Egyptian association lapsed in 1957, but the association was reinstated in 1960; however, its membership was terminated again in 1964. The number of collective members rose to 34 in 1973, 39 in 1982 and 41 in 1994, a level to which it has since remained close.

The further expansion of IPSA's collective membership is reported in table 3.2. In this, as in table 3.1, italicised associations are no longer members; and in the case of a few other associations there has been a break in continuity, since associations may have lapsed and later rejoined, or, in the case of certain countries, the membership of one association has been terminated and it has been replaced by another. Indeed, four countries have seen their representative national association change. IPSA accredited as a collective member a new association for Italy in 1982, for Austria in 1983, for Argentina in 1985 and for Spain in 1994. Names of associations may also have changed over time and, in certain cases, the states to which they belonged may have changed in name or even in geographical identity.

There is a risk that this account will present an exaggerated picture of the commitment of national associations to IPSA. The figures tend to be inflated by the fact that associations that become inactive are typically counted in the total of collective members for several years on the pragmatic grounds that this is mutually beneficial and that it facilitates their re-entry to full membership.

Many of the changes of recent years have been associated with particular political developments, or themselves have a strong political dimension. Thus, as we have seen, IPSA responded pragmatically to internal divisions in Belgium by eventually dealing separately with two associations recognised as representative of the two major communities within the country, and the dissolution of the former Soviet Union, Yugoslavia and Czechoslovakia resulted in recognition of a number of new associations representative of the successor states. A more difficult situation arose in the case of China, which was admitted to membership in 1985 but which withdrew six years later following a dispute about the name under which the Taiwanese association was admitted in 1989 — again, an issue that has proven difficult in many international bodies.

Another interesting development has been IPSA's recognition of regional political science associations. Here, the ground was broken with the recognition of the African Association of Political Science in 1974. At that point, no African national association was a collective member of IPSA, though the Egyptian and Moroccan associations had been members earlier

| Table 3.2: Later collective members | |
|---|---|
| Ceylonese Political Science Association | 1955 |
| Cuban Political Science Association | 1955 |
| Soviet Society for Cultural Relations | 1955 |
| Egyptian Political Science Association | 1956 |
| Norwegian Political Science Association | 1956 |
| Lebanese Political Science Association | 1958 |
| Spanish Association of Political Science | 1958 |
| Swiss Political Science Association | 1959 |
| Argentine Association of Political Analysis | 1961 |
| Danish Association of Political Science | 1961 |
| Czechoslovak Political Science Association | 1964 |
| Pakistan Political Science Association | 1964 |
| Turkish Political Science Association | 1964 |
| Korean Political Science Association | 1967 |
| Bulgarian Political Science Association | 1968 |
| Hungarian Political Science Association | 1968 |
| Romanian Association of Political Science | 1968 |
| African Association of Political Science | 1974 |
| German Political Science Association (GDR) | 1974 |
| Moroccan Political Science Association | 1978 |
| Philippine Political Science Association | 1978 |
| Venezuelan Political Science Association | 1978 |
| Flemish Political Science Association | 1979 |
| Asian-Pacific Political Science Association | 1984 |
| Chilean Association of Political Science | 1984 |
| Chinese Association of Political Science | 1984 |
| Chinese Association of Political Science (Taipei) | 1989 |
| Korean Association of Social Science (Pyongyang) | 1990 |
| Croatian Political Science Association | 1992 |
| Slovenian Political Science Association | 1992 |
| Lithuanian Political Science Association | 1994 |
| Political Studies Association of Ireland | 1994 |
| Slovak Political Science Association | 1994 |
| South African Political Studies Association | 1995 |

and the South African association joined at a later point. In 1984, IPSA recognised the Asian-Pacific political science association based in South Asia, a body whose sphere of interest covered a zone of South Asia not otherwise represented in IPSA.

When considering the order in which the national associations from various countries became members of IPSA, it is apparent that western Europe contributed the largest number of members during the first decade. On the other hand, between 1959 and 1968, the increase came mainly from eastern European countries, though a few more western European countries also joined. It is only during the third decade of the association that membership from third world countries became significant and this trend continued, although on a lesser scale, through into the fourth decade. More recently, political fragmentation in central and eastern Europe resulted in new members from that region.

On the whole, the pattern of recruitment of IPSA's collective members suggests that political science is linked to democracy on the one hand and industrial development on the other. While these may constitute very difficult obstacles to IPSA's expansion, the association remains committed to ensuring that economic impediments to collective membership are reduced, and the new fee structure for collective members adopted in 1997 may encourage the recruitment of new collective members.

*Associate members*

As mentioned above, the concept of associate membership (essentially for academic or other research institutions) has also existed since 1949. The fee for this type of membership was fixed initially at a flat rate of $10 per associate member (though the executive committee reserved the right to increase this should the circumstances of a particular associate member justify a higher rate). This fee was abruptly raised in 1953 to $25, and it remained at this level until 1970, when it was increased to $40. Since then it has increased progressively, to reach $120 by the end of the 1990s. Initially, the attractions of associate membership were limited, and did not extend even to council membership. However, the fact that from the early 1950s it included a free subscription to the *International political science abstracts* and to the *International social science bulletin* (or, later, to the *International social science journal*) was a significant attraction. However, in 1974 this arrangement was ended, and associate members became entitled only to purchase these publications at a discount.

Few associate members joined IPSA during the first ten years of its existence. By 1958, there were only 28 such members. The new secretary general, Serge Hurtig, began to focus on this category of membership, organising a well planned advertising campaign before the 1961 Paris congress (when a substantial sum was spent on advertising). This attracted a large number of associate members; indeed, the number climbed to 58, an increase of 128%. But it is in the period from 1964 to 1967 that the association saw the number of associate members increase the most. The number rose from 68 in 1964 to 194 in 1967, an increase of 185%.

Following this, after a small increase for 1970, the number of associate members fell quickly. Between 1970 and 1973, the association lost 31 members net; it lost 12 between 1973 and 1976, and 47 between 1976 and 1979. Since then, the number has continued to fall steadily (see figure 3.1). The most obvious explanation is the drop in services offered to associate members, and in particular the replacement of free subscriptions to certain publications by small reductions on the regular price. There was also a significance loss when the secretariat moved from Brussels to Ottawa in 1976: 64 associate members did not renew their membership in the following year, and a further 48 followed suit during 1978. As against this, associate members were offered free subscriptions to another attractive publication with the launch of the *International political science review* in 1980. The launch of the *Review* appears, however, to have had limited impact on the long-term drop-off in associate membership. The only exception to the downward trend line occurred in 1994, when generous support from the MacArthur Foundation enabled IPSA to offer complimentary associate membership to a large number of institutions in the transitional democracies of central and eastern Europe.

**Figure 3.1: Associate members, 1952-2000**

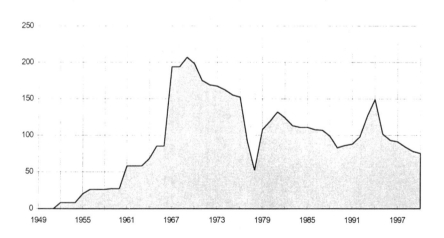

| Table 3.3: Associate members by continent, 1959-99 | | | | | | |
|---|---|---|---|---|---|---|
| Continent | 1959 | | 1979 | | 1999 | |
| | no. | % | no. | % | no. | % |
| Africa | 1 | 3.1 | 1 | 1.0 | 1 | 1.3 |
| America, North | 9 | 28.1 | 28 | 26.7 | 26 | 33.3 |
| America, South | - | 0.0 | 3 | 2.9 | - | 0.0 |
| Asia | 2 | 6.3 | 10 | 9.5 | 8 | 10.3 |
| Europe, East, etc | 1 | 3.1 | 2 | 1.9 | 2 | 2.6 |
| Europe, West | 19 | 59.4 | 60 | 57.1 | 40 | 51.3 |
| Oceania | - | 0.0 | 1 | 1.0 | 1 | 1.3 |
| Total | 32 | 100.0 | 105 | 100.0 | 78 | 100.0 |

There are a number of obvious reasons for the decline in the number of associate members. First, in the late 1960s and early 1970s, IPSA invited several African, Asian and Latin American research institutions to join as associate members, considering that they represented the cores of potential national associations. A number of these did eventually make the transition from associate to collective member status, thus reducing the number of the former. Second, from the mid-1970s onwards, libraries and research institutes in most countries have had to apply serious budgetary restrictions, causing them to terminate their automatic renewal policies in respect not just of associate membership of IPSA but also of other comparable earlier commitments. But there is a third factor: since the launch of the *International political science review* in 1980, IPSA has decided, in deference to its relationship with the publisher of the *Review*, not to seek to expand the number of associate members – and, in particular, not to offer this status to institutions that might be potential direct institutional subscribers to the *Review*.

The geographical distribution of associate members at selected points in time is illustrated in table 3.3. This shows that associate membership has tended to follow a predictable path, with North America and western Europe as the most obvious areas of strength. The latter, indeed, has more or less consistently accounted for over half of all associate members, while the former typically accounts for one third. Outside these continents, only Asia has recorded a significant number of associate members over time.

*Individual members*

Like the other two categories of membership, individual membership also dates from 1949. The subscription level was fixed at that time at $2 for persons who were members of national associations affiliated to IPSA, and $3 for others. In time, the two rates became assimilated, and increased steadily, to $26 in 1980 and to $60 by the end of the century. In 1979 the association implemented a new system of payment for individual members, under which they could take out three-year membership at a reduced rate. In the early stages this facility existed only in congress years, but in 1992 it was extended so that three-year membership could be taken out in any year. In 1981 individual life membership was introduced for retired senior officers of the association and others paying a particular sum.

For a range of reasons discussed already (and especially because of the launch of the *International political science review*, to which all IPSA members receive a complimentary subscription), individual membership has become an increasingly attractive option for political scientists. This is reflected in the steady expansion of this category. From its core of 52 individual members in 1952, IPSA experienced a rapid growth in individual membership until the end of the 1950s. For the next 20 years, as can be seen from figure 3.2, it remained on a plateau of 400-500 members. Then, in the late 1970s, an energetic recruitment drive initiated by the Canadian secretariat under secretary general John Trent pushed individual membership to the levels at which it has since remained. This amounted to a drive to make individual membership the backbone of the association.

Figure 3.2: Individual members, 1952-2000

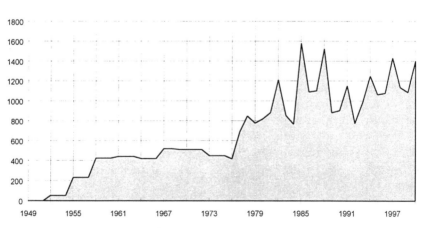

*Note*: The data for 2000 represent the position on 1 July.

| Table 3.4: Individual members by continent, 1959-99 | | | | | |
|---|---|---|---|---|---|
| Continent | 1959 | | 1979 | | 1999 |
| | no. | % | no. | % | no. | % |
| Africa | 4 | 0.9 | 15 | 1.9 | 22 | 2.0 |
| America, North | 236 | 55.8 | 421 | 54.3 | 318 | 29.3 |
| America, South | 8 | 1.9 | 30 | 3.9 | 75 | 6.9 |
| Asia | 28 | 6.6 | 78 | 10.1 | 278 | 25.6 |
| Europe, East, etc | 5 | 1.2 | 12 | 1.5 | 49 | 4.5 |
| Europe, West | 140 | 33.1 | 207 | 26.7 | 309 | 28.6 |
| Oceania | 2 | 0.5 | 12 | 1.5 | 33 | 3.0 |
| Total | 423 | 100.0 | 775 | 100.0 | 1,084 | 100.0 |

Apart from fluctuations between congresses, the number of members doubled in the late 1970s, going from 500 in 1976 to 1,000 in 1979, and subsequently tripled to reach more than 1,500 in 1985. Since then it has levelled off, but the number of individual members in a non-congress year typically remains comfortably above 1,000.

Figure 3.2 also illustrates a very distinctive, "spiky", pattern that has been characteristic of individual membership since 1982: a tendency for membership to peak in congress years and to drop sharply in the two following years (the vertical lines in this figure correspond to congress years). While the high profile of the association during congress years is an obvious explanation for these peaks, there is another factor: a large number of individuals tend to join as one-year members during congress years to take advantage of information then being circulated, and especially to gain from the lower rate at which IPSA members may register for the congress.

A regional breakdown of IPSA membership at three points in IPSA's history is reported in table 3.4. The pattern of western dominance, characteristic also of associate membership, emerges clearly. During its middle years, IPSA attracted very few political scientists from communist and developing countries. But in spite of that, the work of the association was widely disseminated among researchers in communist countries in particular, thanks to the activities of well-developed and well-funded academies and institutes. More recently, it has been refreshing to note the large increase in the number of Asian members. This was especially marked in the case of individual members from Korea, a category that expanded rapidly at the time of the 1997 Seoul congress.

# 4 / SCIENTIFIC MEETINGS

IPSA's scientific activities may be seen as falling into three categories. The first and most visible is the triennial world congress. IPSA's eighteenth world congress takes place in Quebec City in August 2000; by the time it concludes, the pool of political scientists who will have participated in this distinctive form of international meeting will have reached many thousands. In addition, many political scientists have had an opportunity to meet during the round table meetings officially organised by the association (by 1999, more than 40 such meetings had been organised). Third, IPSA has also sponsored a wide range of meetings of other types, most notably through its research committees and study groups. Because of the large volume of activity in the third category, this will be discussed separately in chapter 5. The present chapter thus confines itself to a discussion of world congresses and of round tables planned directly by IPSA.

*World congresses*

World congresses are an integral part of the apparatus of any modern international scientific association. They have been defined in an important study of IPSA's 1979 world congress by two prominent members of IPSA, Richard Merritt and Elizabeth Hanson, as presenting "a broad palette of sessions on a wide range of topics designed to appeal to both the specialist and the generalist, and to people with varying degrees of disciplinary sophistication"; in these respects, they differ from international thematic conferences of experts.[1]

Like the other international unions whose creation was encouraged by Unesco in the late 1940s, IPSA moved quickly to adopt the international congress as its major activity. The year after its foundation, in 1950, it organised its first world congress in Zurich jointly with the new International Sociological Association. Two years later, a larger congress was organised in the Hague in 1952. The normal pattern in international unions is a three, four- or five-year cycle, with a tendency for social science bodies to meet at

---

[1] *Science, politics, and international conferences: a functional analysis of the Moscow political science congress* (Boulder, CO: Lynne Rienner, 1989), p. 1.

shorter intervals than humanities ones; indeed, two-year cycles of world congresses are also to be found.[2] IPSA opted for the triennial cycle, and since 1952 a world congress has taken place every three years (see appendix 5 for further details).

A list of all IPSA world congresses is presented in table 4.1. It will be noticed that the tendency in the early years was for the congress to move between European cities such as Stockholm (1955), Paris (1961), Geneva (1964), Brussels (1967) and Munich (1970). The first congress outside Europe took place in Montreal in 1973. Following a return to Europe (Edinburgh) in 1976, the first congress in eastern Europe took place in Moscow in 1979. Following this, the two later European congresses (Paris in 1985 and Berlin in 1994) were the exception: two congresses took place in South America (Rio de Janeiro in 1982 and Buenos Aires in 1991); one took place in North America (Washington in 1988) and another is planned there (Quebec in 2000); and the first IPSA congress in Asia (Seoul) took place in 1997. Another major landmark is scheduled for 2003, when the first-ever IPSA congress on the African continent takes place in Durban.

The policy of rotating the congress between continents was not designed simply to expose participants to a range of different cultures and national traditions, though that was an important by-product. It became clear at an early stage that a world congress tends to have a very positive effect on political science in the region in which it is held, providing a stimulus not just to academic endeavour but also to efforts to create a local infrastructure to support the discipline.

The Moscow congress of 1979 had an exceptional importance, as we have seen, one whose significance is easy to overlook more than a decade after the collapse of the communist regimes of central and eastern Europe. During the period of the cold war, IPSA had constituted a unique mechanism for contact between those approaching the study of politics from the pluralistic perspective of the west and those who accepted "scientific communism" as the only appropriate mode of social and political analysis.

---

[2] The International Statistical Union holds its congresses every two years; the International Institute of Administrative Sciences, the International Economic Association and the International Association of Applied Linguistics, like IPSA, every three; the International Union for the Scientific Study of Population, the International Geographical Union, the International Mathematical Union, the International Union of Psychological Sciences and the International Sociological Association, every four; and the International Union of Anthropological and Ethnological Sciences, the International Committee for Historical Sciences, the International Federation of Societies of Classical Studies, the International Federation of Philosophy Societies and the International Union of Prehistoric and Protohistoric Societies every five years.

| Table 4.1: World congresses, 1950-97 | | | | | |
|---|---|---|---|---|---|
| No | Year | Date | Location | Papers | Partici-  Coun- |
|    |      |      |          |        | pants    tries  |
| 1. | 1950 | Sep 4-9 | Zurich | 8 | 81 | 23 |
| 2. | 1952 | Sep 8-12 | Hague | 57 | 220 | 31 |
| 3. | 1955 | Aug 21-27 | Stockholm | 25 | 275 | 36 |
| 4. | 1958 | Sep 16-20 | Rome | 77 | 320 | 31 |
| 5. | 1961 | Sep 26-30 | Paris | 59 | 425 | 46 |
| 6. | 1964 | Sep 21-25 | Geneva | 94 | 494 | 43 |
| 7. | 1967 | Sep 18-23 | Brussels | 146 | 745 | 56 |
| 8. | 1970 | Aug 31-Sep 5 | Munich | 259 | 894 | 46 |
| 9. | 1973 | Aug 20-25 | Montreal | 324 | 1,044 | 56 |
| 10. | 1976 | Aug 16-21 | Edinburgh | 327 | 1,081 | 56 |
| 11. | 1979 | Aug 12-18 | Moscow | 450 | 1,466 | 53 |
| 12. | 1982 | Aug 9-14 | Rio de Janeiro | *825 | 1,477 | 49 |
| 13. | 1985 | Jul 15-20 | Paris | *600 | 1,763 | 66 |
| 14. | 1988 | Aug 28-Sep 1 | Washington | *890 | 1,265 | 74 |
| 15. | 1991 | Jul 21-25 | Buenos Aires | *870 | *1,400 | *55 |
| 16. | 1994 | Aug 21-25 | Berlin | *660 | 1,884 | 73 |
| 17. | 1997 | Aug 17-21 | Seoul | *621 | 1,470 | 72 |

*estimates

The location of a political science congress in Moscow was on the one hand a novel experience for scholars from the west; but it also had a profound effect in legitimising the discipline (however defined) in states run by communist governments, and it led to considerable organisational developments.

The Moscow congress also represented the maturing of the world congress in terms of numbers of participants. As table 4.1 shows, by then a plateau of approximately 1,500 had been reached. The first congress attracted only 81 participants, but, for many years subsequently, the numbers increased steadily. The second Paris congress (1985) was very different from the first (1961); the number of participants reached its first peak at 1,763. Since then, only the Berlin congress (1994) exceeded this, with 1,884 participants.

The number of participating countries varies rather more from one congress to the next, and the region in which they are concentrated varies to an even greater extent. The number of countries represented increased steadily up to 1988; since then, it has normally been a little in excess of 70.

It would be refreshing to be able to record that congress participants were drawn proportionally from all the regions of the world, or even in proportion to the strength of the discipline in the various regions, but IPSA has been no more successful in attaining equity of regional representation than other international scientific associations, and, indeed, it is only in an ideal world that geographical representation of this kind could exist. Two general biases have typically been present: a tendency for West European and North American scholars to be over-represented, and a tendency towards exceptionally high participation from the region in which the congress is held.

The number of papers presented at IPSA world congresses fluctuated greatly during the first two decade of the association, though there was a general tendency for it to increase. The increase really took off in the 1970s; in recent congresses, the number of papers actually presented has typically been comfortably in excess of 600. Interestingly, precisely as the number of papers has increased, so too has the difficulty of establishing precise information about the actual number. Essentially, we have three sources of information, though they might be better described as indicators: first, the congress programme; second, the book of abstracts of congress papers; and, third, the actual collection of congress papers itself. Unfortunately, but predictably enough in a major international event of this kind, these three indicators can lead to radically different estimates, but the last of them is probably the most accurate.

In terms of intellectual structure, IPSA congresses fall into two relatively clearly defined categories, with the Montreal congress of 1973 forming a bridge between them. The first eight congresses were organised around a number of discrete topics. There were three such topics in 1950, and the number rose to nine by 1967, before dropping to four in 1970. Each addressed a rather specific issue within the discipline, and efforts were made to ensure that coherence was maintained by appointing a rapporteur in respect of each topic.

As the numbers of papers submitted in respect of each topic expanded, however, it became increasingly difficulty to maintain this structure. IPSA's response was to expand the number of topics but to group them under two main themes. Thus, in the 1973 Montreal congress Stein Rokkan acted as convenor in respect of 12 sessions on the theme "Politics between economy and culture", while Karl Deutsch acted as convenor for the remaining eight sessions on the theme "Key issues in international conflict and peace research".

This development left the way open for an alternative approach: a single over-arching theme used as an umbrella for a large number of topics. Under Jean Laponce's presidency, the Edinburgh congress of 1976 was the first to have an overall theme ("Time, space and politics"), and this policy was also followed in 1979 and 1982 ("Political science: peace, development and knowledge" and "Society beyond the state in the 1980s", respectively). Because of the big increase in the number and variety of papers and the sheer scale of the event, an effort was made to streamline the academic organisation of the congress. For the 1985 Paris congress, it was agreed to adopt a rather specific theme ("The state: evolution and interaction with national and international society") and a more rigid limit was set on the number of sessions in all categories of meetings.

Since then, debates on quality versus broadening, fragmentation versus uniformity, or disciplinary rigour versus regional representation have continued to animate meetings of the association's programme committee. As in the case of other international scholarly bodies, there is a serious financial dimension to these debates, since participants typically have to present a paper if they are to receive travel support, and this tends to increase the number of papers. Following the Paris meeting, themes have tended once again to be rather broad. They have included "Towards a global political science" (1988), "Centres and peripheries in contemporary politics: interdependence and power asymmetries" (1991), "Democratisation" (1994) and "Conflict and order" (1997).

Alongside this evolution in the thematic orientation of IPSA world congresses, a second development has contributed to a further change in the significance of these meetings. As early as 1964, meetings of groups of specialists, which later on became "research committees" and "study groups", were added to the congress programmes. In 1970, there were already as many as 187 papers presented to such meetings, whereas only 70 were related to the theme of the congress. Furthermore, starting with the 1976 congress, the voice of the members was heard strongly by means of a series of gatherings called "special meetings" or "exceptional meetings" that were suggested by individual members and which had themes with an international appeal.

At the 1988 Washington congress, a fourth category of papers was added under the heading of "sessions on research in progress" in order to foster international exchange of information on current research that is not related to the themes of the other section of the programme. This category was later absorbed by existing categories, or by one of two new categories that made their appearance at the 1994 Berlin congress: reviews of the state of the discipline, and sessions with a particular regional appeal.

Thus, each congress typically has had four categories of activities, in addition to a small number of plenary sessions: (1) panels dealing with the theme, organised by the programme committee; (2) research committee and study group panels; (3) special sessions proposed and organised by individual members; and (4) other sessions, possibly of rather disparate kinds, including such areas as the state of the discipline or regional issues. Finally, it should be noted that advantage is properly taken of attendance at world congresses by people who wish to organise other meetings for purposes unconnected with the congress. These are usually listed in the congress programme as a courtesy under the title "concurrent meetings".

Each congress nevertheless tends to have its own particular flavour. For example, the 1985 congress theme was subdivided along the usual lines: theoretical analysis, comparative research and international problems. On the other hand, the 1988 Congress had an "umbrella" theme (the global-isation of the discipline) which covered a series of "mini-plenary" sessions while providing the general thrust to the other sections dealing with the main areas of research in political science. Further experimentation took place in Berlin in 1994 and in Seoul in 1997, with innovative attempts to tap distinctive local perspectives. Thus, there seems to some extent to be a de-compartmentalisation of the format of the congress; much depends on the position taken by the programme chair and the local organisers.

The organisational arrangements that lie behind this series of world congresses rest on two supports — the local organising committee and the programme committee. Whereas other international associations leave all the organisational tasks to the committees of the congress host countries, IPSA maintains its right itself to organise its academic programme, as we have seen. Though relieved of this burden, the local organisers still face a formidable task, and it is only through their commitment that the associa-tion's congress series has been able to flourish.

The funds needed to organise a congress have increased steadily over time. Whereas only $3,500 was needed for the first congress, the amount was already six times higher for the 1961 congress, namely $20,339. The 1970 Munich congress cost $67,013, or 19 times the amount of the first con-gress. In 1982, the Rio de Janeiro congress cost $145,523, or forty times the cost of the 1950 Zurich congress. Costs since then have tended to rise fur-ther, though much depends, of course, on the general cost of living in the city where the congress is being organised.

The financing of congresses has become a key element for the health of the association and international political science. The method of financing is rather unique. From the outset, it has been recognised that in order to organise meetings that are international in character, that is with a minimum representation of IPSA member countries from the first, second, and third worlds, the association has to be able to underwrite the travel costs of a large number of political scientists and to offer speaking opportunities to satisfy the "active participation" requirements of the national agencies that subsidise the researchers.

In many countries there is either a shortage of foreign currency or a reluctance towards financing social science researchers and especially political scientists (or sometimes both). For this reason, IPSA requires every country that is host to one of its congresses to provide a fixed amount in order to finance the local organisation and as much as possible of the travel expenses. Furthermore, Robin Hood style, congress participants are asked to pay moderately high registration fees (although they are lower than for most international conferences), which are then used for a travel grant scheme, constituting in effect a form of cross-subsidy. Especially in earlier years, Unesco has provided generous support to congress participants. Through these three sources of financing, IPSA has been able to provide travel expenses for many political scientists from mostly third world countries to attend several of the past congresses. In addition, the local organisers are sometimes able to raise large sums for additional travel grants (this was especially the case in 1994 and 1997).

It is appropriate to conclude this discussion of the world congress and the philosophy underlying it by quoting at length from the opening address of the 1985 programme chair, the late Francesco Kjellberg:

> One of the main objectives of each of our congresses is *to contribute to the strengthening of the comparative aspects of our discipline*. By bringing together colleagues from institutions world-wide, we invite them to compare either different experiences or their perceptions of similar experiences. ... The vitality of every discipline depends on this relentless questioning of the assumed. This questioning is precisely what a world congress gathering specialists from all over the world is for. ...
>
> In my view, a world congress must also have a second role — *to remind us of the unity of political science*. ... A congress such as ours is by necessity based on the idea that in spite of its apparent fragmentation, in spite of the centrifugal forces at work, political science must keep its unity. ...
>
> A world congress must have a third function: *the rejuvenation of political scientists*. ... Thus, the stars of our discipline as well as those who still have to build their reputation attend our congresses. By its very size and its diversity, the

congress establishes a climate of equality: for a week, we are all equal — or almost equal. The congress is an opportunity that everybody can take advantage of if they so desire.

There are, of course, other functions that I will only list: the congress allows us to meet old friends and colleagues in pleasant surroundings; it allows us to strengthen our own sense of identity, establish new contacts, make new friends, and even gossip.

## Round table meetings

Many international scholarly organisations comparable with IPSA rely entirely on the activities of specialist research committees to fly the disciplinary flag between congresses, but others follow a definite programme of inter-congress activities. A number of these organisations mount large-scale events between congresses, either on a global or on a regional basis, using the designation "roundtable", "symposium" or "conference" for this. In some cases, the timing, location and format of these events appears to be rather ad-hoc; on others, a systematic programme is followed.

Since its foundation, IPSA has made modest efforts to follow the model of inter-congress round tables. Apart from the numerous round table meetings sponsored by other bodies but supported by IPSA, those to which it has sent representatives or those organised by its research committees and study groups (an average of ten a year), the association has organised a major round table meeting to coincide with executive committee meetings. Guidelines for the organisation of meetings of this kind were drawn up by Asher Arian and secretary general John Trent, and approved by the executive committee at meeting no. 44, Rio de Janeiro, 7-8 August 1982; these were incorporated, with further revisions, in IPSA's current guidelines for inter-congress activities approved at meeting no. 73, also in Rio de Janeiro, on 6-8 March 1997.

Round table meetings have typically taken place annually. The first such meeting was planned in 1949 for the following year, but it finally took place only in 1952 in Cambridge. A five-day round table on the theme of the teaching of political science was used as the occasion for a meeting of the IPSA executive committee, and this set the pattern for future round table meetings.

By early 2000, a total of 44 meetings of this kind had taken place. These are listed in appendix 6. It will be noticed that almost all of the earlier meetings (those organised before 1980) took place in Europe. It is not without significance — given the atmosphere of the cold war and its impact on the social sciences — that five of these were arranged in communist-run countries: two in Yugoslavia (Opatija in 1959 and Dubrovnik in 1975), two in Poland (Jablonna in 1966 and Krakow in 1977) and one in Romania (Bucharest in 1972). Only five took place outside Europe: two in the United States (Pittsburgh in 1957 and Ann Arbor in 1960), one in Brazil (Rio de Janeiro in 1978), one in Israel (Jerusalem in 1974) and one in India (Calcutta in 1979).

The themes selected tell us much about the preoccupations of IPSA during this period. In the early years there was a particular concern with establishing the autonomy of the discipline, and therefore with developing an appropriate teaching infrastructure. Many of the roundtable meetings were multi-thematic, focusing on several areas of central concern. An especially striking feature is the tendency for the themes to be of particular interest to the region in which the meeting was held, reflecting IPSA's long-standing concern to stress its relevance to local political circumstances.

The character of round table meetings changed considerably in the late 1970s. First, there was a tendency for the themes to become more specialised, reflecting the maturing character of the discipline and the shift in emphasis away from the basic questions that had preoccupied political scientists in the 1950s. Second, the meetings tended to become more frequent and shorter, reflecting the deepening infrastructural development of the discipline: the organisation of IPSA became more professional, requiring more frequent meetings of the executive committee, and falling barriers to physical communication facilitated this. Third, and most importantly, the significance of this round table series was greatly diminished as IPSA began to recognise specialised research committees, and increasingly looked to them to sustain academic momentum between congresses.

The increased frequency of the meetings and the decline in the traditional dominance of western Europe emerge clearly when we consider the period from 1980 onwards. Indeed, only five of the 24 meetings during this period took place in western Europe. Central and eastern Europe accounted for seven: one each in Yugoslavia (Zagreb, 1985) and Poland (Warsaw, 1991), not surprisingly given the traditional strength and independence of the social sciences in these countries, one in the Soviet Union (Moscow, 1988) and two in the tightly-controlled German Democratic Republic (Weimar, 1980, and Berlin, 1987). Two further meetings took place after the definitive fall of communism, in the Czech Republic (Prague, 1995) and in Poland (Krakow, 1999).

The growing importance of Asia has been no less striking: six roundtable meetings have taken place there, in Japan (Tokyo, 1982 and Kyoto, 1994), Korea (Seoul, 1990), India (Madras, 1992), Taiwan (Taipei, 1995) and

Israel (Jerusalem, 2000). Finally, four meetings have taken place in North America (Urbana-Champaign, 1983; Ottawa, 1986; Chicago, 1992; and Quebec, 1998) and two in South America (Buenos Aires, 1986 and Rio de Janeiro, 1997).

Certain predictable features are associated with the themes that have emerged in the more recent round tables. Increased specialisation in the discipline is reflected in the narrower topics that have been selected. This specialisation is also encouraged by the particular needs of the host institution. Thus, it is not surprising to find a focus on the capacity of government to cope with urgent social problems in Florence in 1984, on causal relations between the state, politics and economy in Seoul in 1990, or on the transition to democracy in eastern Europe in Warsaw in 1991. Such meetings have helped to raise the profile of the discipline and of IPSA in the region where they have been held, and are of benefit both to IPSA and to the hosts themselves.

The number of participants and the number of countries represented at each round table meeting vary considerably. Several factors seem to come into play, as for example the topic, the budget available, the international tensions of the times and the distance to the host country. On average, 42 participants from 16 countries attended round table meetings held during the first 20 years of the association, and the pattern appears to have changed little since then.

# 5 / RESEARCH AND PROFESSIONAL DEVELOPMENT

All international scholarly associations rely for a great deal of their scholarly achievements, especially between congresses, on the contribution of standing groups of various kinds that are dedicated to tackling systematically particular issues within the discipline and that enjoy a degree of continuity over time. IPSA, too, has followed this model, and the first part of this chapter looks at the operation of its research committees and study groups. In the second part we look at other activities that have a semi-permanent existence, notably a commitment to encouraging the work of younger scholars.

*Research committees and study groups*

From the beginning of the 1970s, the research committees and study groups officially recognised by IPSA have played an important role in the scientific activities of the association. These groups, which bring together political science specialists interested in the advancement of knowledge on a particular topic of international interest, have been responsible for numerous round table meetings and exchanges amongst experts, as well as publications. They are an important element in IPSA's success in its search for ways of stimulating the development of political science world-wide because they are at the forefront of research and encourage the creation of international networks of researchers with similar interests.

Although gatherings of specialists debating particular topics appeared as components of the programme as early as the Geneva congress in 1964, it is only with the 1970 Munich congress that steps were taken to institutionalise these gatherings by establishing permanent research committees.

The new concept was endorsed by the association in order to promote long-term collaboration between experts from different countries and with common interests in certain areas of political science. More specifically, the research committee, although it can be dissolved, is a permanent structure bringing together specialists wanting to launch transnational comparative research in order to expand theory and increase knowledge on a topic often of international interest.

| Table 5.1: The first research committees, 1970-76 | | |
|---|---|---|
| RC 1 | 1970 | Conceptual and terminological analysis |
| RC 2 | 1972 | Political elites |
| RC 3 | 1971 | European unification |
| RC 4 | 1972 | *Latin American political studies* |
| RC 5 | 1972 | Comparative studies on local government |
| RC 6 | 1970 | Political sociology |
| RC 7 | 1971 | *Quantitative and mathematical approaches to politics* |
| RC 8 | 1972 | Legislative development |
| RC 9 | 1973 | Comparative judicial studies |
| RC10 | 1973 | *Peace and conflict studies* |
| RC11 | 1975 | Science and politics |
| RC12 | 1975 | Biology and politics |
| RC13 | 1976 | *Development and political systems* |
| RC14 | 1976 | Politics and ethnicity |

In 1970 IPSA extended recognition to two groups that also enjoyed research committee status in the International Sociological Association: one on conceptual and terminological analysis (also recognised by the International Social Science Council) and one on political sociology. Recognition of a further 12 groups followed quickly; these covered major subfields or topics within the discipline (such as the legislature, the judiciary, local government and elites) as well as topics with a geopolitical reference point (such as European unification and Latin American politics) and those dealing with the interface between politics and other disciplines (such as biology and science in general). These groups are listed in table 5.1 (in this, as in tables 5.2 and 5.3, committees or groups in italics no longer exist; it should be noted that the name originally approved may have changed subsequently).

In 1976 IPSA recognised a second type of body, also comprising scholars engaged in research on a specific topic: the study group. Very quickly, this became the main route to research committee status: groups wanting to become research committees had to serve a probationary period, normally of several years, as study groups. In effect, the stage called "study group" allowed specialists to be officially recognised internationally, thus increasing their number of contacts and raising their standing more generally. This recognition and the resulting fairly stable structure permitted the development of long-term research programmes. It also allowed IPSA to ascertain whether the research topic was of sufficient interest to the inter-

| Table 5.2: Study groups awarded research committee status, 1978-98 |
|---|
| RC15  1978   Political geography (SG 1, 1976) |
| RC16  1978   Socio-political problems of pluralism (SG 5, 1976) |
| RC17  1978   The emerging international economic order (SG 8, 1977) |
| RC18  1979   Asian political studies (SG 2, 1976) |
| RC19  1979   Sex roles and politics (SG 3, 1976) |
| RC20  1979   Standards of political conduct (SG 4, 1976) |
| RC21  1979   Political education (SG 9, 1976) |
| RC22  1984   Global communication (SG 5, 1980) |
| RC23  1986   Political support and alienation (SG 3, 1977) |
| RC24  1986   Armed forces and society (SG 7, 1981) |
| RC25  1986   *Marxist political thought (SG 9, 1981)* |
| RC26  1987   Human rights (SG 4, 1980) |
| RC27  1987   Structure and organisation of government (SG20, 1984) |
| RC28  1987   Comparative federalism (SG21, 1984) |
| RC29  1987   Psycho-politics (SG10, 1981) |
| RC30  1988   Political attitudes (SG13, 1982) |
| RC31  1988   Analytical political philosophy (SG15, 1983) |
| RC32  1988   Public policy analysis (SG14, 1982) |
| RC33  1989   Comparative sociology of political science (SG11, 1982) |
| RC34  1989   Comparative representation and electoral systems (SG24, 1986) |
| RC35  1990   Technology and development (SG 6, 1981) |
| RC36  1991   Political power (SG17, 1983) |
| RC37  1991   Rethinking in political development (SG16, 1983) |
| RC38  1991   Politics and business (SG22, 1984) |
| RC 7  1992   Women, politics and development (SG30, 1988) |
| RC 4  1993   Public bureaucracies in developing societies (SG27, 1986) |
| RC10  1994   Global policy studies (SG31, 1989) |
| RC13  1994   Democratisation in comparative perspective (SG32, 1989) |
| RC25  1997   Comparative health policy (SG19, 1984) |

national community and thus whether the group would be able to play an efficient role if it became a research committee. A list of study groups that have made the transition to research committee status appears in table 5.2.

Of course, especially in more recent years a number of study groups have wished to remain in this category rather than being promoted to research committee status. In time, the principal feature (other than title) distinguishing study groups from research committees became the fact that the former were allocated two panels at IPSA world congresses and the latter one panel. A list of study groups that retained this status appears in table 5.3. Given the near-erosion of the de facto distinction between these two categories, the executive committee decided in 1999 to approve the merger of the two: all remaining study groups were given research committee status, and in future the route to research committee status would be via a probationary period.

The creation of the research committees and study groups allowed IPSA's academic objectives to be addressed from a position rather different from anything that the IPSA executive committee would be able to organise: it facilitated a level of decentralisation, specialisation and continuity in activities that no all-purpose executive committee could be expected to sustain. During general gatherings organised by IPSA (such as congresses and round table meetings), specialists have a tendency to intervene along individualistic and ad-hoc lines, whereas meetings organised by the research committees and study groups promote to a much greater extent a spirit of long term cooperation. This marshalling of expertise is calculated to yield more substantial and tangible results than meetings of specialists at congresses and other meetings of a general character, and thus is likely to contribute more substantially to IPSA's mission.

It would be difficult to overestimate the contribution of research committees and study groups to the attainment of IPSA's academic mission. In addition to their enormous contribution to IPSA congresses, most are extremely active between congresses, organising round table meetings and other events, engaging on collaborative research projects often through subgroups, issuing newsletters and publishing books, articles and monographs. A number of research committees now even publish their own journals, and maintain web pages that provide an effective channel of access to particular topics within the discipline.

In the course of the 1970s, to ensure that research committees and study groups did not become too self-focused, IPSA sought to define systematically the process and the criteria that would allow it to recognise officially only those groups that conformed to the goals that pursued by IPSA. While this process was characterised initially by an attitude of flexibility towards regulations, but this perspective has been gradually replaced by a stricter attitude towards enforcement of the rules.

In 1980, after several years of study and debate on the topic, the *Rules governing the organisation and functioning of research committees and study groups* were endorsed by the executive committee. These required, inter alia, that each group that wished to be officially recognised must represent as equally as possible all the areas of the world, and reflect the different schools of thought. Similar provisions were made in respect of the steering

| Table 5.3: Study groups, 1976-99 |

| | | |
|---|---|---|
| SG 1 | 1976 | Politics and law |
| SG 2 | 1976 | Comparative political ideas |
| SG 8 | 1981 | Political science in developing countries |
| SG10 | 1982 | Constitution making as a political process |
| SG12 | 1982 | Repression and representation: convergent trends between Latin America and Europe |
| SG13 | 1982 | Political values and norms |
| SG18 | 1983 | Theories of the state |
| SG23 | 1984 | Constitution making as a political process |
| SG25 | 1986 | Religion and politics |
| SG26 | 1986 | Politics, institutions, performance and evaluation |
| SG28 | 1987 | Executive structures and roles in contemporary government |
| SG29 | 1987 | Military rule and democratisation in the third world |
| SG33 | 1989 | Quantitative international politics |
| SG34 | 1992 | Politics of global environmental change |
| SG 1 | 1992 | The welfare state and developing societies |
| SG 2 | 1992 | Public enterprises and privatisation |
| SG 3 | 1994 | New world orders |
| SG 4 | 1995 | Geopolitics |
| SG35 | 1995 | Local-global relations |
| SG36 | 1995 | Administrative culture |
| SG37 | 1995 | Socialism, capitalism and democracy |
| SG 5 | 1996 | System integration of divided nations |

board of each, and there was a requirement for turnover in its membership. These measures were designed to ensure that research committees and study groups would be open both to the recruitment of members from a wide variety of backgrounds and that none would be captured by any exclusive orthodoxy. A committee on research committees and study groups was created to monitor activities in the area in 1979 (it was renamed the commission on research committees and study groups in 1982, and, with broadened terms of reference, the committee on research and training in 1998).

The relationship between IPSA and its research committees and study groups has not been confined to regulation of the latter by the former. The idea of a meeting between representatives of research committees and study groups and the commission charged with responsibility for monitoring their activities was initiated in the 1980s. In 1988 this body asked for a larger measure of financial assistance from IPSA, and the IPSA executive committee agreed at its meeting no. 58 in Oslo, 22-23 August 1989, to provide a modest subsidy for their activities. This was finally implemented in 1990.

Under this scheme, members joining IPSA were invited to indicate their support for up to two research committees and study groups; the IPSA secretariat would transfer $3.00 to the committees or groups in question in respect of each member indicating a preference for support of this kind. This experiment turned out to be only partially successful. It was extremely expensive to administer; it resulted in very small transfers, or none, to many groups; and it did not necessarily result in the admission of the individual IPSA members who had indicated their wish to support particular groups to membership in these groups. For these reasons, a new system of financial support was initiated in 1999. Under this a larger overall sum is being made available, and from this a smaller number of larger grants will be made on the basis of applications from research committees themselves.

*Professional development and other activities*

While the world congress has always been IPSA's most visible activity, it will be clear from the above account that it has also sought to pursue a vigorous programme of inter-congress activities. For its first two decades of existence, the most important of these activities were the round table meetings that took place in each of the inter-congress years. Since 1970, while these meetings have continued, they have been eclipsed by the work of research committees and study groups.

But this is not the whole story. From the very beginning, IPSA has also organised other kinds of meetings, often in cooperation with a national association or another international organisation, on topics of significance for the discipline. Although it is difficult to provide a precise listing of meetings of this kind because of difficulties of classification, by 1988 at least 20 such gatherings (often referred to as "promotional round tables") had taken place. Many of these were highly innovative: on the political participation of women (organised by Maurice Duverger in Paris in 1953), for instance, or on political models and national development (organised by Karl Deutsch in Rio de Janeiro in 1969).

Although IPSA has not discontinued its interest in activities of these kinds, it is clear that the need for such intervention has diminished as the role of research committees and study groups has increased. For this reason, IPSA has instead begun to devote attention to a new area, that of professional development, and especially the introduction of younger scholars to contemporary developments in political research.

Already in the 1960s three events were organised under this general heading: a seminar in Bombay, India, in 1964 on the twin themes of political leadership and public opinion, propaganda and communications; a similar seminar in Kampala, Uganda, in 1964 on the theme of political and administrative aspects of the economic activities of the state; and a two-stage seminar in New Delhi, India, in 1966 and 1967 on the theme of political theory and behaviour.

A further inter-congress initiative was the organisation of so-called "travelling workshops" targeted especially at younger scholars in regions in which the discipline was most in need of development. This idea was first placed on IPSA's agenda at executive committee meeting no. 49 in Zagreb, 14 March 1985, and, following further discussions at later executive committee meetings, a formal proposal was drawn up by Richard L Merritt and accepted at executive committee meeting no. 55 in Moscow on 21-22 March 1988. This did not incorporate a set of detailed guidelines, but it included a summary of the purpose of the workshops drawn up by secretary general John Trent.

The first "workshop" meeting took place in Tallinn, Estonia, on 3-9 January 1993, and was organised with the support of Unesco. The theme was "Elections and party systems in contemporary democracies", and it was attended by 70 professors, local and regional government officials and journalists from all over the former Soviet Union. The second meeting was held in Vilnius, Lithuania, on 10-15 December 1996. The designation of the meeting was changed to "international symposium" to reflect more accurately the underlying purpose of the initiative. The theme was "The challenge of regime transformation: new politics in central and eastern Europe", and the meeting was again well atended. The third symposium took place in Durban, South Africa, on 26-29 January 1999, and consisted of a seminar organised jointly by IPSA and the African Association of Political Science on the theme "Globalisation and the future of nations and states". The most recent meeting of this kind took place in Patiala, India, in collaboration with IPSA's RC14 (Politics and ethnicity) on 6-9 January 2000. An international conference on "Ethnicity in the first world, the third world and ex-communist countries", organised by the Department of Correspondence Courses, Punjabi University, Patiala, was followed by a special programme on recent developments in the discipline and on the state of political science in India.

# 6 / PUBLICATIONS

For any international scholarly body, the development of a sizeable stable of publications is a central activity. Especially in the social sciences, this activity acquires additional importance from the imperative to promote cross-national contact and communication. Thus, shortly after its foundation, the International Sociological Association launched its journal *Current sociology* (1952), and in addition to other book publications it launched a book series in 1974 in which approximately 50 volumes had appeared by 2000.

Not surprisingly, then, IPSA became involved from its very beginnings in the development of new research tools of this kind for political science specialists. The association is, indeed, bound by one of its formal objectives, as defined in article 5 of its constitution, to facilitate the spread of information about developments in political science. It is also required by the same article to publish books and journals and to provide a newsletter for its members. The present chapter considers IPSA's publishing activities, grouping these into five categories.

The first area to be considered, chronologically but not only in this sense, is IPSA's article abstracting service, the *International political science abstracts*, which dates from 1951 and constitutes IPSA's longest-standing contribution to the development of the discipline. The second category was a similar one, the *International bibliography of political science*, launched shortly after the *Abstracts*. The third area is the IPSA journal, launched in 1980 as the quarterly *International political science review*. Fourth, from its earliest years IPSA has been involved in book publications, and its activities in this area were later systematised in the shape of a book series. The final area is that of internal communication. With a view to providing information to its members, IPSA launched a quarterly newsletter in 1953. This was replaced in 1977 by a bulletin that appears three times a year, *Participation*. In the concluding section of this chapter we consider IPSA's remaining in-house publications.

In reviewing these developments, we will be concerned mainly with activities planned centrally by IPSA. It should, however, be noted that quite apart from publications issued or sponsored by IPSA itself, IPSA's research committees and study groups have been extremely active in publishing. A complete overview of these activities is beyond the scope of this article, but a superficial survey of this very important area is nevertheless incorporated in the section dealing with book publication.

## The International political science abstracts

One of the most important decisions of IPSA's founding conference in 1949 was to agree on "the establishment on a modest scale of a documenting and reference service for members of the association".[1] This moderately ambitious undertaking to fill one of the most obvious lacunae in the infrastructure of the discipline turned out to be the seed of one of IPSA's greatest success stories. This initiative was designed to tackle the growing gap between the rapidly expanding volume of material being published in political science and related disciplines and the capacity of scholars to keep track of these publications. The reality was that it was becoming increasingly difficulty for researchers to compile comprehensive bibliographies in their fields of interest.

It is true that some bibliographical aids existed at this point. The *International index* had begun publication in the United States in 1907 and the *Subject index to periodicals* in Great Britain in 1915, but these spanned a very wide range of journals and were not for the specialist.[2] The *Public Affairs Information Service bulletin* began publication in 1915 on a modest scale, but it was only towards the end of the century that it began to be widely used by political scientists.[3] In 1931 the London School of Economics had begun publication of the *London bibliography of the social sciences,* which continued with multiannual supplements and then with annual supplements down to the end of the 1980s (see below). This focused mainly on books. Those interested in periodical literature in political science could turn to the *Bulletin bibliographique de documentation internationale contemporaine,* which was published in Paris from 1926 to 1940 and continued after 1946 as the *Bulletin analytique de documentation politique, économique et sociale.*[4] The *Social sci-*

---

[1] "International Political Science Association: summary report of the constituent conference held at Unesco House, 12-16 September 1949", *International social science bulletin* 1 (3/4) 1949, p. 84.

[2] These later became, respectively, the *Social sciences and humanities index* (1957-74) and the *Social sciences index* (1974-), and the *British humanities index* (1963-).

[3] This is now the Public Affairs Information Service; for a description, see http://www.silverplatter.com/catalog/pais.htm.

[4] The index as it then stood was published in the late 1960s by GK Hall of Boston as part of their bibliographical series.

*ences citation index* was then well in the future, being launched only in 1973.[5]

This was the context of IPSA's two interventions in the area of documentation and bibliography. With the support of Unesco and of the newly created International Committee for Social Science Documentation (ICSSD), IPSA responded to the dearth of bibliographical documentation with two initiatives. The two had in common the fact that their administrative headquarters were located in the Fondation Nationale des Sciences Politiques in Paris, that they were sponsored and indeed published by Unesco, that they were compiled under the auspices of the ICSSD, and that they were supervised by Jean Meynaud, Secretary General of IPSA from 1950 to 1955. These were the *International political science abstracts* and the *International bibliography of political science.*

The *Abstracts* were launched in 1951 under the editorship of Jean Meyriat, director of documentation services at the Fondation Nationale des Sciences Politiques and secretary general of the ICSSD. The new periodical was a quarterly one, based entirely on abstracts of articles in political science. The pattern adopted in 1951 has since been adhered to. The editor reviews articles from specialised or general periodicals and journals as well as the main yearbooks dealing with political science, and publishes non-critical abstracts. The articles published in English have an abstract in English; those published in other languages have an abstract in French (since 1977, all the titles have had an English translation). The abstracts now derive from three sources: those published in the journals themselves as summaries of the articles, those provided by authors on request from the editor, and those drawn up by the editor or editorial staff (who also have to edit and summarise many of the lengthier abstracts provided by authors or journals). To complete the process of assisting researchers, each issue contains a detailed subject index. This is incorporated in an annual subject index, and is supplemented by an annual author index.

What has made the *Abstracts* a particularly useful resource over the years has been its system of classification. The main areas of the discipline as identified in 1951 reflected conventional thinking at the time. They have been retained ever since, constituting a remarkably stable framework for documentary research. This classification system is summarised in table

---

[5] See http://www.isinet.com/; also in the future was *POL-DOK: Politische Dokumentation*, a monthly collection of abstracts of German-language periodical literature in politics that began publication in 1966 — but this is now in the past, since it has discontinued publication.

---

**Table 6.1: Classification system of the**
*International political science abstracts*, **1951-99**

I-  Political science: method and theory

II- Political thinkers and political ideas

III- Governmental and administrative institutions
   a) central institutions
   b) state, regional and local institutions

IV- Political process: public opinion, attitudes, parties, forces, groups and
   elections

V-  International relations
   a) international law, organization and administration
   b) foreign policy and international relations

VI- National and area studies

Note: there have been minor terminological changes over the years. This table reports
the wording in 1999.

---

6.1. Although there have been minor changes in terminology over the years, this basic pattern remains unaltered.

Jean Meyriat, the founding editor of the *Abstracts*, continued as editor until 1963. He was succeeded by Serge Hurtig, then secretary general of IPSA (1961-67), who has continued in this role until the present. The editors have been assisted from the outset by a small editorial board, which was once operational (editors in the United Kingdom and the USA provided abstracts from journals published in their countries) but which became mainly advisory. After 1963 Serge Hurtig took over almost all of the tasks performed by assistant editors and the publication became very much a one-person operation.

Initially, the *Abstracts* were published directly by Unesco, with IPSA and the ICSSD as sponsors. After four years, however, the project was sufficiently well established to be handed over to a commercial publisher, and Blackwell of Oxford was given responsibility. Blackwell published the series from volume 5 (1955) to volume 23 (1973). At that point, on the recommendation of editor Serge Hurtig, IPSA decided to assume direct responsibility for publishing. This arose mainly from a desire to match the growing volume of political science output by increasing the frequency of appearance of the publication and speeding up the whole process. Beginning with volume 24 (1974), the *Abstracts* have appeared six times per year. In this context, speed of production acquired increasing importance, and removal of the distinction between the editorial, printing and publishing processes was considered appropriate. IPSA has since retained full control of the finances, including subscription rates.

Following a period of stability until the end of the 1960s, during which the number of abstracts appearing annually was typically less than 1,500, a huge expansion took place in the early 1970s: the number of abstracts increased from approximately 2,200 in 1970 to more than 5,000 in 1975, and it has since climbed steadily above this level. The pattern of expansion is indicated in table 6.2, and reflects the explosion in political science journal literature dating from the 1970s and the effort of the editor to be as comprehensive as possible.[6]

Two further developments should be noted. First, beginning in 1982 (in association with the IPSA triennial world congress of that year) a new triennial series has been launched — a special edition collecting the abstracts of papers presented at IPSA congresses.

Second, a more far-reaching development took place in 1995. At that point, under the terms of a contract with major CD-rom reference publishers SilverPlatter, the *Abstracts* became available on CD-rom, and were later made available also on the internet. This was an inevitable development not only in terms of the intrinsic desirability of facilitating electronic access but also with a view to asserting the leading role of the *Abstracts* in an increasingly computerised world. The SilverPlatter database at present comprises more than 76,000 abstracts going back to 1989, and its significance as a research tool increases steadily.[7]

IPSA's main preoccupation with the *Abstracts* has always been to provide a service to the international political science community. In addition to direct assistance from Unesco, IPSA itself subsidised the *Abstracts* heavily for many years (mainly through funds earmarked by Unesco). Between 1973 and 1977 IPSA was able to reduce its own contribution gradually, a change made possible by the shift to direct publication by the association itself and the dedicated efforts of editor Serge Hurtig, who filled an important role not just in the academic domain but also in that of publishing and management. With the ending of the IPSA subsidy in 1977, the *Abstracts* continued to enjoy a small subsidy from Unesco, but this, too, ended in 1987. Since then, the *Abstracts* have been entirely self-financed; indeed,

---

[6] For a review of the circumstances associated with this expansion, see Serge Hurtig, "Developments in the world of political science journals", pp. 271-6 in Eberhard Bort and Russel Keat, eds, *The boundaries of understanding: essays in honour of Malcolm Anderson* (Edinburgh: University of Edinburgh Press, 1999).

[7] For further information, see http://www.silverplatter.com/catalog/ipsa.htm.

| Table 6.2: *International political science abstracts*: abstracts and journals, 1951-99 | | |
|---|---|---|
| Year | Abstracts | Journals reviewed |
| 1951 | 1,447 | 111 |
| 1955 | 1,502 | 145 |
| 1960 | 1,461 | 168 |
| 1965 | 1,471 | 184 |
| 1970 | 2,206 | 353 |
| 1975 | 5,015 | 810 |
| 1980 | 5,133 | 853 |
| 1985 | 5,846 | 933 |
| 1990 | 5,990 | 944 |
| 1995 | 6,404 | 981 |
| 1999 | 7,434 | 992 |

they have made a substantial and growing contribution to IPSA's reve-
nues. Given the much greater flexibility of electronic media and the low
physical costs associated with them, it is likely that IPSA's income from
this source will continue to be healthy in the years to come.

## The International bibliography of political science

IPSA's second initiative in the area of documentation complemented the
*Abstracts*. This was the launch of a full bibliographical service, extending
not just to journal articles but also to books and national and international
documents, a project endorsed at the Hague congress of IPSA in 1952. Car-
ried out by the ICSSD, it began publication as a yearbook entitled the *International bibliography of political science* in 1953. The first volume covered
material published during the year 1952, and this pattern was subsequently adhered to.

The *Bibliography* is a selective inventory of titles of important books,
publications and articles in the field of political science that have been
published during the year. It does not contain any abstracts, but adopted a
policy of cross-referring to those published in the *International poltical science abstracts*. It is selective in that it only reports on scientific studies (such
as books, articles and official government publications), thereby excluding
material of an ephemeral or controversialist nature. But it also imposes its
own scientific standards, and covers studies of general interest rather than

those which focus on particular characteristics of a country and that might therefore be of lesser interest for foreign readers. Its classification system follows the same major headings as the *Abstracts*, though its much greater number of references permits use of a more elaborate set of subheadings.

The founding editor of the *Bibliography* was IPSA secretary general Jean Meynaud, and its first three volumes were described as being "prepared by the International Political Science Association in cooperation with the International Committee for Social Science Documentation". Although Meynaud continued as editor from volume 4 (1955) to volume 8 (1959), the acknowledgement reversed this relationship over this period, attributing primary responsibility for the compilation to the ICSSD. Beginning with volume 9 (for 1960), its name was changed to *International bibliography of the social sciences: political science*, reflecting its role as one of the four major bibliographical series sponsored by Unesco. The others were in economics (1952-), sociology (1951-) and social and cultural anthropology (1955-).

Also starting with volume 9 (1960), Jean Meyriat, secretary general of the ICSSD, began his long term as editor, and he continued in this capacity until volume 35 (1986). During all of this period, the *Bibliography* continued to appear "under the auspices of the International Political Science Association". The role of IPSA in respect of the *Bibliography* after 1955 was much less significant than in the case of the *International Political Science Abstracts*; it became reduced in effect to the presence of an IPSA representative on the *Bibliography's* editorial committee.

Initially published directly by Unesco, once the venture became securely established it was handed over to a commercial publisher. This began with volume 9 for 1960, which was published by Stevens and Son (later Tavistock) in London and Aldine in Chicago; Routledge took over from volume 34 (1985). A major development in the history of the *Bibliography* took place in the late 1980s. With a view to attaining economies of scale and greater speed of production, the entire publication project was taken over by the British Library of Political and Economic Science (the library of the London School of Economics and Political Science, LSE), which assumed responsibility for all four bibliographical series. At the same time, the library discontinued its own long-standing series, the *London bibliography of the social sciences*, the last volume of which (47) appeared in 1989. Volume 36 of the *Bibliography* (for 1987) was thus not merely a continuation of the old series but also of the LSE bibliography; and IPSA's role was no longer even a token one.

Although the coverage of the *Bibliography* was initially necessarily more extensive than that of the *Abstracts*, its rate of growth was much more restrained. This reflected not any stagnation in the rate of production of the material covered but rather an increasingly selective approach. Thus, volume 1 (covering 1952) contained 4,246 items; following some increase and occasional peaks, the corresponding number for volume 46 (covering 1997) was 5,491 items. But the significance of this collection is rather greater than indicated by these numbers: in 1995 the entire four-series set went on line, retrospectively to the very beginning, and it now comprises a massive database holding more than 1,700,000 references to journal articles, book reviews, monographs and selected book chapters. Over 90,000 new references are added each year, and the collection is also available on CD-rom.[8]

*The International political science review*

Following its foundation, IPSA's primary concern was with congress organisation rather than publication: it depended both on its collective members, the national political science associations, and on a range of other publishing outlets to edit and produce professional journals to service the needs of the discipline. In its early years, IPSA could rely on the Unesco quarterly journal, the *International social science bulletin*, founded in 1949, both to provide news about developments within the association and to publish papers presented at IPSA's congresses. Beginning with volume 11 (1959), the *Bulletin* was rechristened the *International social science journal*. Since it did not produce a journal itself, IPSA distributed first the *Bulletin* and then the *Journal* to individual members at a reduced rate as one of the benefits of membership. This relationship persisted even after IPSA launched its own journal: right up to the present, IPSA offers a facility by which members may avail themselves of a reduced-rate subscription to the *International social science journal*. The *Journal*, incidentally, is now published in six languages: English, French, Spanish, Arabic, Chinese and Russian (see http://www.unesco.int/issj/ index.htm).

IPSA had also planned from the outset to produce its own "international political science review", interestingly anticipating the title that would later be adopted. But implementation of this proposal took more than 20 years.[9] The immediate origins of IPSA's journal lie in the world congress that took place in Edinburgh in 1976. In addressing the council meeting,

---

[8] For further information see http://www.lse. ac.uk/IBSS/.

[9] The French title mentioned in 1949, *Revue internationale des sciences politiques*, was, in its use of the plural, slightly different from the name finally adopted; see "Association Internationale de Science Politique: rapport résumant les travaux de la conférence constitutive tenue à la Maisonde l'Unesco du 12 au 16 septembre 1949", *Bulletin international des sciences sociales* 1 (3/4), 1949, p. 90.

outgoing president Jean Laponce suggested the establishment of an international political science journal as an outlet for the best work of members of the association, and he was mandated to investigate the feasibility of this, to approach prospective publishers and to make recommendations to the executive committee. In addition to the option of a commercial publisher, which would require a subsidy from IPSA, an alternative was also considered: a form of in-house publication that would entail joint sponsorship by IPSA and its research committees but which might prove even more costly. At its meeting in Rio de Janeiro on 23-26 August 1978, the executive committee endorsed the first option, and a contract was signed with Sage Publications, Inc., of Beverly Hills to publish a quarterly journal.

The first issue of the new journal, the *International political science review*, appeared at the beginning of 1980. Its editor, John Meisel, defined its target audience as the international political science community, and emphasised the centrality of this dimension:

> Our hope is that this focus will ensure its escape from one of the major weaknesses of much of current political analysis—the worse for being ubiquitously overlooked—namely, the crippling consequences of parochialism. It is remarkable that even journals which aggressively espouse comparative methodologies all too often do so within an ethnocentric and/or narrow ideological conceptual apparatus and with similarly restricted sources of data.

The *Review's* objective was also to counteract the effects of an ever increasing specialisation that threatened to divert interest away from global analyses, which consider the discipline as a whole and address the whole of human experience. It has thus focused on the promotion and the dissemination of broadly based analysis, eschewing any internal disciplinary or other biases.

In addition to the editor, a small editorial committee was established (this increased from five members in 1980 to eight in 1999) together with an advisory board (comprising 15 members in 1980 and rising to 30 by 1999, drawing heavily on current and former members of the IPSA executive committee). John Meisel was joined as co-editor in 1986 by Jean Laponce and in 1995 by Nazli Choucri. He stood down the following year, and the *Review* has since been edited by Nazli Choucri and Jean Laponce. Having more than one editor made it possible to dispense with the services of a paid assistant editor and greatly reduced the cost of the operation, since the editors are not remunerated.

**Table 6.3: Selected thematic issues of the**
*International political science review*

**Vol 1, 1980**

Richard L Merritt, *Studies in systems transformation*

Francesco Kjellberg and Henry Teune, *Recent changes in urban politics: national-local linkages*

Jerzy J Wiatr, *Political ideology: its impact on contemporary political transformations*

Jean Gottmann and Jean Laponce, *Politics and geography*

**Vol 5, 1984**

Bahgat Korany, *Foreign policy decisions in the third world*

Jean Laponce, *Freedom and boundaries*

Mattei Dogan, *Political crises*

Hugh G Thorburn, *Pluralism and federalism*

**Vol 10, 1989**

Elizabeth W Marvick, *Case studies in psychopolitics*

SN Eisenstadt, *The historical framework of revolutions*

Hugh G Thorburn and Jordi Solé Tura, *Pluralism, regionalism, nationalism*

**Vol 15, 1994**

Torbjörn Vallinder, *The judicialization of politics*

Roger D Masters, *Human nature, biology, and justice*

**Vol 20, 1999**

William M Lafferty, *The pursuit of sustainable development: concepts, policies and arenas*

Javier Santiso, *States and markets: essays in trespassing*

Urs Luterbacher, *New developments in international institutions and organizations*

From the outset, the *Review* adopted a distinctive approach to the challenge of combining breadth of scope with intellectual focus by relying on guest-edited thematic issues. The capacity of the *Review* to reconcile thematic variety with intellectual rigour is indicated in the variety of themes taken up. Table 6.3 illustrates the scope of the topics that have been tackled in selected years since the launch of the *Review*. Beginning with volume 8 in 1987 a more flexible approach was adopted: a fourth issue in each volume was made an "open" one, in which articles appear that are not necessarily grouped by any theme. The success of the *Review* is reflected in the fact that by 1997 it was among the top 20 journals worldwide in terms of its "impact factor" as measured by the *Social science citation index*.

Although the language of the great majority of contributors to the *Review* is clearly English, its bilingual character is underscored not just in its title (*Revue internationale de science politique*) but also in the fact that each article is also abstracted in the other language — articles written in French also have an English abstract, and vice versa.

In terms of publication arrangements, the initial contract with Sage, Inc., lasted for the first seven volumes. In subsequent years the production of the journal was transferred to other publishers: to Butterworth of Guildford, England (beginning with volume 8 in 1987) and to Sage of London (beginning with volume 17 in 1996). With each move the number of words per issue was increased substantially and the financial arrangements improved from IPSA's perspective. The competition among publishers for having the *Review* is a measure of its academic and commercial success. Its attractiveness to IPSA members (to whom it is distributed free as one of the benefits of membership) has been a central feature in the maintenance of IPSA's high number of individual members.

Articles in the *Review* are, of course, included in the collections of the major indexing services: *ABC Pol Sci*, *CARL Uncover*, *Current contents / social and behavioral sciences*, *International bibliography of political science*, the *Social science citation index*, and the *Social sciences index*. Abstracts are included in the *Political science abstracts*, *Sociological abstracts* and, of course, the *International political science abstracts*, as well as in a range of more specialised publications, including *Electoral Studies*; *Linguistics and language behaviour abstracts*; *Middle East abstracts and index*; *Peace research abstracts*; *Periodica Islamica*; *Social planning/policy and development abstracts*; *Southeast Asia abstracts and index*; and *US political science documents*.

The *Review* has also made a very successful transition to the world of electronic publishing. At Sage's suggestion, it became one of a few journals participating in the so-called SuperJournal experiment at the University of Manchester beginning in 1997. This consisted of putting selected journals from major British publishers online in electronic format with hypertext and multimedia linkages. The journals were clustered into subject categories, and a powerful search engine was made available.

Electronic publishing policy has subsequently taken a rather different direction, however. Beginning in 1999, Sage began to offer the *Review* in both print and electronic formats for a single subscription rate. This means that any library subscribing to the *Review* from 1999 onwards also has access to the electronic version through intermediaries approved by the publisher. IPSA has sought to protect the interests of print-only readers by arranging that subscriptions to the electronic version can not be purchased separately from the print edition, thus ensuring the future of the latter.[10]

As in the case of the *Abstracts*, of course, the *Review* began its life as a service to the academic community rather than as a commercial venture. In both cases, indeed, IPSA initially invested heavily, and committed substantial financial resources to ensuring the success of these publications. Happily, like the *Abstracts*, the *Review* turned out to be a commercial success story.

### *Publication of books*

The explicit sponsorship of a book series did not feature early on the IPSA agenda. Nevertheless, it was inevitable that the large volume of material prepared for IPSA congresses and round table meetings would seek an outlet. For the most part, the initiative rested with individual IPSA members who made publishing arrangements independently of IPSA. In many cases, papers presented at IPSA meetings appeared as collections of essays, were incorporated in such collections, or were published in various journals, either independently or as special issues.

In this context, the *International social science bulletin* and later the *International social science journal* were of particular importance. In 1960, for instance, the first three issues of the *International social science journal* were based on papers edited on behalf of IPSA by, respectively, Stein Rokkan (on "Citizen participation in politics"), Jean Meynaud ("The social sciences and peaceful cooperation") and CB Macpherson ("Technical progress and political decision"). This tradition has continued, the *Journal* frequently building a special issue around papers presented at IPSA world congresses. Up to the 1960s, the other journals in which material originating in IPSA activities most commonly appeared were the *American political science review* and the *Revue française de science politique*. Since then, as the volume of IPSA-sourced output has increased, so too has the range of journals publishing it.

In the 1950s, IPSA was responsible for major projects in association with Unesco, which published the resulting documents. These are listed in table 6.4, and they illustrate the central role that IPSA was already beginning to play in the cross-national study of political life. IPSA subsequently spon-

---

[10] The publishers also maintain a web page that provides tables of contents and abstracts from vol. 18 (1997) onwards; it may be consulted at http://www.sage pub.co.uk/journals /details/j0034.html.

---

**Table 6.4: Early IPSA books**

*Unesco series*

WA Robson, *The university teaching of social sciences: political science* (Paris: Unesco, 1954) [also published in French as *Les sciences sociales dans l'enseignement supérieur: science politique*]

Maurice Duverger, *The political role of women* (Paris: Unesco, 1955) [also published in French as *La participation des femmes à la vie politique*]

Benjamin Akzin, *New states and international organizations* (Paris: Unesco, 1955)

*Various publishers*

Gunnar Heckscher, *The study of comparative government and politics* (London: George Allen & Unwin, 1957)

Harold Zink with Arne Wåhlstrand, Feliciano Benvenuti and R Bhaskaran, *The comparative study of rural local government in Sweden, Italy and India* (London: Stevens & Sons, 1957)

Henry W Ehrmann, ed., *Interest groups on four continents* (Pittsburgh: University of Pittsburgh Press, 1960)

Jan Barents, *Political science in western Europe* (London: Stevens & Sons, 1961)

Austin Ranney, ed., *Essays on the behavioral study of politics* (Urbana: University of Illinois Press, 1962)

Henry Maddick, *Democracy, decentralisation and development* (London: Asia Publishing House, 1963)

*Atherton Press series*

Harold W Lasswell, *The future of political science* (New York: Atherton Press, 1963)

JE Hodgetts, *Administering the atom for peace* (New York: Atherton Press, 1964)

*Elsevier series*

Hayward Alker, Karl W Deutsch and Antoine H Stoetzel, eds, *Mathematical approaches to politics* (Amsterdam, London, New York: Elsevier, 1973)

Dusan Sidjanski, ed., *Political decision making processes* (Amsterdam, London, New York: Elsevier, 1973)

---

sored the publication of edited collections or syntheses based on its round table meetings.

Among *syntheses* (in which a rapporteur based his or her report on a set of individual papers presented at a meeting) we may note Gunnar Heckscher's analysis of the comparative study of politics, based on IPSA's third round table meeting in Florence in 1954, and Jan Barents's trend report on political science in western Europe, based on IPSA's sixth round table meeting in Opatija in 1959. Examples of *edited collections* are Henry Ehrmann's comparative study of interest groups, based on IPSA's fifth round table meeting in Pittsburgh in 1957, and Austin Ranney's study of behavioural approaches, based on IPSA's seventh round table meeting in Ann Arbor in 1960.

It will be noted that IPSA turned to a range of publishers in these cases. The fact that two volumes were published by Stevens and Son of London, with whom IPSA was also associated through the *International bibliography of political science*, and that these were explicitly published "under the auspices of the International Political Science Association", was a pointer to the direction that IPSA was now to take. In the early 1960s it entered into a contractual arrangement with Atherton Press of New York for a book series. The contract was, however, cancelled in 1964 after the appearance of only two volumes. A further effort in this direction was made ten years later, when a contract was signed with Elsevier of Amsterdam, but this, too, proved to be of relatively short duration.

It was only in the 1980s that IPSA finally launched an ongoing book series entitled *Advances in political science: an international series*. The executive committee and council gave approval for this project in 1979, to be pursued in association with Sage publications. Richard L Merritt was appointed general editor of the series, and a small editorial committee was established in 1981. The series was launched in 1982 with two books. As the series editor noted in his introduction, the new project was animated by the same core concern as the *International political science review*: the need to counteract tendencies towards parochialism and overspecialisation. The new series was designed to present the best work then being produced:

(1) on the central and critical controversial themes of politics and/or (2) in new areas of enquiry where political scientists, alone or in conjunction with other scholars, are shaping innovative concepts and methodologies of political analysis.

Within the first five years of the series, five volumes had appeared. A sixth volume was published by Butterworth in 1987 as part of a once-off arrangement, and a contract was signed with Cambridge University Press in the same year. Three further volumes appeared under the terms of this contract.

When the contract with Cambridge ended in 1991, the search for a new publisher began under a new book series editor, Itzhak Galnoor. Although a number of promising lines of enquiry were followed, including one for a

**Table 6.5:** *Advances in political science*: first series

*Sage Ltd, London*

1. Harold K Jacobson and Dusan Sidjanski, eds, *The emerging international economic order: dynamic processes, constraints and opportunities* (1982)

2. Daniel Frei, ed., *Managing international crises* (1982)

3. Charles Lewis Taylor, ed., *Why governments grow: measuring public sector size* (1983)

4. Richard L Merritt and Anna J Merritt, eds, *Innovation in the public sector* (1985)

5. Claudio Cioffi-Revilla, Richard L Merritt and Dina A Zinnes, eds, *Communication and interaction in global politics* (1987)

*Butterworth, London*

6. John R Schmidhauser, ed., *Comparative judicial systems: challenging frontiers in conceptual and empirical analysis* (1987)

*Cambridge University Press, Cambridge, UK*

7. Herbert Alexander, ed., *Comparative political finance in the 1980s* (1989)

8. David M Olson and Michael L Mezey, eds, *Legislatures in the policy process: the dilemmas of economic policy* (1991)

9. Peter Wagner, et al, eds, *Social sciences and modern states: national experience and theoretical crossroads* (1991)

series dealing with "basic concepts" in political science, it was decided to proceed slowly until such time as an arrangement could be made with a publisher that took full account of IPSA's interests.

A satisfactory contract was achieved in 1995 with Macmillan of London, negotiated by the new book series editor, Asher Arian. By the end of 1999 five books had appeared in the relaunched series, and contracts have been signed for several others (the titles that have appeared to date are listed in table 6.6).

It should not be assumed that this account of IPSA's book series is in any way a comprehensive overview of the association's contribution to the production of books in political science. There are two other areas that we need to consider: the publication of books outside the formal ambit of IPSA sponsorship but nevertheless emanating from IPSA-initiated activities, and the enormous output of IPSA's research committees and study groups.

In the first category we find a line of articles and books (including both monographs and edited collections) dating back to the 1950s. It is worth pointing out that a core element in Maurice Duverger's seminal work *Les partis politiques* (1951) received its first airing at IPSA's Zurich congress in 1950, and was published in the *International social science bulletin* (volume 3, no 2, 1951, pp. 314-52) as "The influence of electoral systems on political life". Many works—such as those associated with the names of Stein Rokkan and Karl Deutsch—that were subsequently to be elevated to classic status within the profession originated in the same way.

Not surprisingly, IPSA was also indirectly responsible for major surveys of the discipline, ranging from William G Andrews's *International handbook of political science* (Greenwood Press, 1982), which IPSA supported though it did not formally sponsor, to Robert E Goodin and Hans-Dieter Klingemann's *New handbook of political science* (Oxford University Press, 1996), based substantially on papers presented at IPSA's Berlin congress in 1994.

In the case of the second category, the output of research committees and study groups, it is difficult to do anything more than to scratch the surface. A complete listing of their publications would not be possible in a publication of this kind, and a partial listing would be invidious; but it is appropriate to attempt at least to illustrate the volume and diversity of their contribution to the discipline. We may do this, in an historical account of this kind, by means of an arbitrary selection: a listing of some of the earliest books published by the oldest of IPSA's research committees. Table 6.7 lists one early book publication in the case of each surviving re-

---

**Table 6.6:** *Advances in political science*: new series

*Macmillan, London*

Klaus von Beyme, *Transition to democracy in eastern Europe* (1996)

Christa Altenstetter and James Warner Bjorkman, eds, *Health policy reform, national variations and globalization* (1997)

Frank P Harvey and Ben Mor, eds, *New directions in the study of international conflict* (1998)

Henry J Jacek and Justin Greenwood, eds, *Organized business and the new global order* (1999)

Ofer Feldman, *The political personality of Japan: analysing the motivations and culture of freshman Diet members* (1999)

Klaus von Beyme, *Parliamentary democracy: democratization, destabilization, reconsolidation, 1789-1999* (2000)

---

**Table 6.7: Selected early publications of IPSA's oldest research committees**

RC1 Fred W Riggs, ed., *Ethnicity: INTERCOCTA glossary: concepts and terms used in ethnicity research* (Honolulu: University of Hawaii, 1985)

RC2 Mattei Dogan, ed., *The mandarins of Western Europe: the political roles of top civil servants* (Beverly Hills: Sage, 1975)

RC3 Ghita Ionescu, ed., *The new politics of European integration* (Basingstoke: Macmillan, 1972)

RC6 Richard Rose, ed., *Electoral behaviour: a comparative handbook* (New York: The Free Press, 1974)

RC8 GR Boynton and Chong Lim Kim, eds, *Legislative systems in developing countries* (Durham, NC: Duke University Press, 1975)

RC9 John R Schmidhauser, ed., *Comparative judicial systems* (London: Butterworth, 1987)

RC11 André Philippart, ed., *Ordre et désordre en politique scientifique* (Bruxelles: Symposium Fondation Francqui, 1979)

RC12 Albert Somit, ed., *Biology and politics: recent explorations* (Paris: Mouton, 1976)

RC14 Dennis L Thompson and Dov Ronen, eds, *Ethnicity, politics, and development* (Boulder, CO: Lynne Rienner, 1986)

RC15 Jean Gottmann, ed., *Centre and periphery: spatial variation in politics* (Beverly Hills: Sage, 1980)

RC16 Stanislaw Ehrlich and Graham Wootton, eds, *Three faces of pluralism: political, ethnic, and religious* (Farnborough: Gower, 1980)

RC17 Harold K Jacobson and Dusan Sidjanski, eds. *The emerging international economic order: dynamic processes, constraints and opportunities* (Beverly Hills: Sage, 1982)

RC19 Margherita Rendel, with Georgina Ashworth, ed., *Women, power, and political systems* (New York: St Martin's Press, 1980)

RC21 A Bodnar and W Goehring, eds, *Different aspects of political education* (Warsaw: Centralny Osrodek Metodyczny Studiow Nauk Politycznuch, 1981)

Note: the original RCs 4, 7, 10 and 13 have been replaced. Two items in the above list (under RC9 and RC17) appear also in table 6.5.

---

search committee recognised by IPSA before 1980.

This list of course fails to do justice to the full book output of these research committees in their early years and *a fortiori* to their subsequent output of books, not to mention the very large number of journal articles

and other publications for which these and other IPSA research committees and study groups have been responsible. Most produce and circulate
their own newsletters, the more substantial of which amount almost to
mini-journals. In addition, many research committees produce directories
of members or of experts, and registers of research. More recently, many of
them have established their own web pages.

Even more impressively, a number of research committees are or have
been connected, in varying degrees of closeness, with book series or journals. Thus RC12 has been linked with the book series *Research in biopolitics*
(Greenwich, CT: JAI Press), five volumes of which had appeared by 1997,
and RC40 has pursued a similar link in connection with a series on *New
regionalisms* (Aldershot: Ashgate Publishing). Among research committees
that are or have been linked with particular journals we may mention
RC14 with *Nationalism and ethnic politics* (London: Frank Cass); RC21 with
*Politics, groups and the individual: international journal of political psychology
and political socialization* (Nordersted: APP GmbH); RC27 with *Governance:
an international journal of policy and administration* (Oxford: Blackwell); RC28
with *Publius: the journal of federalism* (Easton, PA: Lafayette College); and
RC38 with *Politics and business* (London: Carfax).

*Participation*

As already mentioned, in its early years IPSA was able to rely on the
Unesco quarterly journal, the *International social science bulletin*, not only as
an outlet for academic work but also as a mechanism for reporting news
about the association and its activities. Inevitably, as the *Bulletin* focused
increasingly on academic publication rather than organisational reporting,
IPSA found it necessary to establish its own organ for internal circulation.
This took the form of a newsletter.

The first number of the IPSA news circular accordingly appeared in
January 1953, and it continued to be published three or four times a year
until 1965. Two issues appeared in 1966 and, after a gap, the last issue appeared in April 1969. Over its lifespan, the news circular performed an
invaluable service to IPSA, especially as its membership expanded and the
need for communication grew. Its 46 issues increased in size from five
pages (no. 1, 1953) to 57 pages (no. 46, 1969). Its average length over this
period was 18 pages.

At its meeting in Edinburgh in August 1976, the executive committee
authorised the new IPSA secretary general, John Trent, to re-establish the
IPSA newsletter. The proposal was that this would be edited initially from
the secretary general's office by the new IPSA administrator Liette

| Table 6.8: Content of *Participation*, 1995-99 |
| --- |
| • Features |
| • IPSA news (including world congress features) |
| • News from national associations |
| • News from research committees and study groups |
| • Report (seasonal): |
|   1-IPSA individual and associate members; |
|   2-directory of research committees and study groups; |
|   3-directory of national associations |
| • Other news |
| • In memoriam |
| • Book corner |
| • Forthcoming events |

Boucher, and then by an outside editor. In practice, responsibility for editing the newsletter has since remained with the secretariat.

The first issue of the new newsletter, *Participation*, appeared in January 1977. In its opening editorial, the secretary general outlined the purpose behind this new initiative, one that has remained central ever since:

> The basic objective of *Participation* is to provide information in three topic areas: about the IPSA itself; concerning the internationally relevant activities of political scientists; and basic material on national and regional political science associations.

Since then, the newsletter has appeared regularly three times each year. It has continued to report on the same kind of material over the years: activities within IPSA, including news of its research committees and, later, study groups; information on various events sponsored by or associated with IPSA; details on publications of potential interest to IPSA members; and advance notice of forthcoming events, meetings or conferences. Beginning with volume 2 (1978) and up to volume 12 (1988), an additional fourth "special" issue was also published. This was an "information supplement", containing systematic documentation on research committees and on national and regional political science associations. Every three years, one of the "regular" issues was replaced by a special congress issue in which the preliminary congress programme appeared.

A further restructuring took place beginning with volume 19 (1995). The executive committee authorised a new format in accordance with which material would be grouped in more systematically organised sections, and all material would be retyped rather than being reproduced photographically. This new format is summarised in table 6.8.

| Table 6.9: Feature articles in *Participation*, 1995-99 | |
|---|---|
| The organisation of political science in the Czech Republic, | |
| by Jan Škaloud | 19(2), 1995 |
| The organisation of political science in Slovakia, | |
| by Silvia Mihalikova | 19(2), 1995 |
| Political science in Austria, by Peter Filzmaier, | |
| Otmar Höll and Thomas Weninger | 19(3), 1995 |
| The United Nations Fourth World Conference on Women: | |
| report from Beijing, by Jane Bayes | 19(3), 1995 |
| IPSA's lining and kitchen: some very personal remarks, | |
| by Stanislaw Ehrlich | 19(3), 1995 |
| Political science in Russia: formation and development, | |
| by Michael Marchenko | 20(1), 1996 |
| The vote for the State Duma: a report from Russia, | |
| by Luigi Graziano | 20(1), 1996 |
| Political science and the Human Dimensions Programme, | |
| by Arild Underdal | 20(1), 1996 |
| Seoul: site of the XVIIth IPSA world congress, by Dalchoong Kim | 20(2), 1996 |
| The conflict early warning systems research programme, | |
| by Hayward R Alker | 20(3), 1996 |
| Teaching politics in Russian universities, by Helen Shestopal | 21(1), 1997 |
| The International Social Science Council: an overview | 21(2), 1997 |
| Supply and demand of social science information, | |
| by Arnaud F Marks | 21(2), 1997 |
| IPSA president, 1997-2000: Theodore J Lowi, by Michio Muramatsu | 21(3), 1997 |
| IPSA past-president, 1994-1997: Jean Leca, by Theodore J Lowi | 21(3), 1997 |
| Political science in Spain, by Jacqueline J Polanco | 22(1), 1998 |
| Political science in Hungary, by Máté Szabó | 22(2), 1998 |
| Globalization, political science, democracy: report on a visit to Japan, | |
| by Theodore J Lowi | 22(3), 1998 |
| Political science in Poland, by Krzysztof Palecki | |
| and Czeslaw Mojsiewicz | 22(3), 1998 |
| Fifty years of IPSA: 1: organisational development | 23(1), 1999 |
| Fifty years of IPSA: 2: scientific activities | 23(1), 1999 |
| IPSA at the world conference on science, Budapest, | |
| by Theodore J Lowi and Rainer Eisfeld | 23(2), 1999 |
| Fifty years of IPSA: 3: publications | 23(3), 1999 |

Aside from more clearly defined sections, a more vigorous (but imperfectly successful) effort was made to commission articles dealing with aspects of the profession, which appeared as longer feature articles. These covered such topics as the development of political science within particular countries, international academic developments of potential interest to IPSA members and aspects of IPSA's history. A list of those appearing from 1995 to 1999 is included in table 6.9.

Another feature of the new restructuring was the introduction of a seasonal "report" section. Each year since 1995, the first issue of *Participation* has included a detailed report on individual and associate membership. The report in the second issue of each year has incorporated IPSA's directory of research committees and study groups, originally published independently but now updated and reproduced annually. The report in the third issue has comprised a directory of national and regional political science associations. This expanded content leaves no space for the special issue dealing with the preliminary congress programme; hence, a special fourth issue containing this has appeared in each pre-congress year (1996 and 1999).

The new format permitted a very considerable expansion in content for little additional direct cost. The average number of words per issue increased from about 10,000 in 1994 to more than 30,000 from 1995 onwards, though the number of pages increased only slightly. The physical appearance of the bulletin was altered in 1995 with a new cover design, and, again, with professional assistance, in 1996.

*Other publications*

From the beginning, IPSA has also made available a large volume of internally published material. Initially, this appeared in the form of papers reproduced photographically or by analogous means from typescript. Thus the papers presented at IPSA's second round table meeting in Paris in 1953 were made available in this form, and this tradition was subsequently adhered to.

The growing cost of paper reproduction and problems of storage led to a further development. Beginning with the Edinburgh world congress in 1976, the practice began of making a set of microfiche copies of all congress papers available for sale to IPSA members and others. This practice was continued up to the Berlin congress in 1994. Technological development permitted a more flexible approach to be taken in the case of the Seoul congress of 1997: this time the papers were stored on CD, greatly facilitating ease of access. In each case, a descriptive booklet containing an index of congress papers has also been produced.

Beginning with the 18th meeting in Krakow in 1977, the papers presented at IPSA's annual round table meetings were also made available on microfilm. This practice continued up to the 34th meeting in Madras in

---

**Table 6.10: IPSA's publications in microform,
1976-97**

World congress papers (fiche): XI congress, Edinburgh, 1976 – XVI congress,
Berlin, 1994: 6 sets; from 104 to 250 fiches in each set

World congress papers (CD-rom): XVII congress, Seoul, 1997: one set; 2 CDs

IPSA roundtable meetings (fiche): 18th meeting, Krakow, 1976 – 34th meeting,
Madras, 1992: 15 sets; from 4 to 18 fiches in each set

Research committee and study groups inter-congress meetings, 1977-90 (fiche):
44 sets; from one to 22 fiches in each set

---

1992. It was decided at that point to discontinue this policy, since the costs
were far greater than the revenue generated by a trickle of sales. From 1978
to 1990 the papers presented at inter-congress round table meetings of research committees and study groups were also made available on microfiche by the secretariat. After a slow start, the volume of sales increased
significantly, but a later drop-off in interest caused this series also to be
discontinued. A summary of IPSA's microfiche publications is included in
table 6.10.

In addition to publications that are essentially for the record and that are
produced in small numbers, such as those mentioned above, IPSA also
produces other publications for specific purposes. The triennial congress
programme, produced by the local organisers of each congress, is an obvious example. In 1992, the chair of the commission on research committees
and study groups, Pippa Norris, produced a booklet entitled *Directory of
research committees and study groups*, providing detailed information on
each group. Since 1995 this has been incorporated in *Participation*, but a
second stand-alone edition was published in 1996. In 1997 a second booklet entitled *The International Political Science Association: an introduction* was
published. This provided information on IPSA's history, organisation, activities and publications, and included a directory of national political science associations. Other publications issued from time to time include
leaflets of various kinds in English and French, which cover such areas as
general information on IPSA, information on research committees and
study groups, guides to publications and information on executive committee members.

# 7 / CONCLUSION

It would be an exaggeration to describe IPSA as an organisation that arose simply out of the ashes of the second world war. Yet, as we have shown in this short history, the circumstances of its birth were political in the fullest sense, and the horrors of the physical and human destruction of much of the world, together with a sense of shock at what had been revealed about the potential for inhumanity within the very core of political leadership, were still fresh in the minds of all those involved. As IPSA's first president, Quincy Wright, put it at the very first meeting of the new association,

> The conditions which have brought our Association into existence are the corruption of politics by inhuman tyranny and total war which have brought and may again bring disastrous consequences to all sections of the world. The purpose which inspires our Association is to eliminate these corruptions by the universal application of scientific method in dealing with political problems.[1]

It would be difficult to imagine a more difficult programme, or a more noble objective. President Wright was himself the first to admit the extent of the challenge. He continued his address by asking a question that had been posed for half a century, and that would still be posed a half a century later, but on the answer to which there is still no agreement: "is a science of politics possible?". For Wright and his far-seeing colleagues, the answer lay in rejecting the incompatibility of art and science.

The focus of much of IPSA's subsequent work might lead the observer to conclude that sight had been lost of its grand objective. Its constitution, after all, defined its fundamental purposes much more modestly, and the day-to-day work of the association implied a more overt concern with the route to professional organisational development than with the path to world peace. The formation of national political science associations was encouraged, dialogue and debate in world congresses and smaller scale round table meetings was promoted, bibliographical and abstracting services were launched and systematic efforts were made to offer a publishing forum to facilitate communication between political scientists. As the asso-

---

[1] Quincy Wright, "The significance of the International Political Science Association: opening address", *International social science bulletin* 3 (2), 1951, p. 276.

ciation matured, an impressive network of standing research committees and study groups developed, and the association began publication of a journal that was quickly to establish a reputation as being among the most authoritative within the discipline.

In these activities, IPSA was treading a well-worn path that was familiar to many international scholarly bodies. But even a cursory analysis of the output of other international federations in the social sciences and the humanities will show that, from this comparative perspective, IPSA has been exceptionally successful in making its mark on the global community of scholars that constitutes its target support base. It might well be the case that other long-term global forces would have helped to break down barriers to international communication, but IPSA has certainly speeded this process along. Large strides in the intellectual development of the discipline might well have grown from the work of various networks of scholars, but IPSA can claim a large amount of credit for facilitating and encouraging this. The findings of political science research might easily have found other mechanisms to achieve wider dissemination, but IPSA promoted the idea of publication from an early stage; its formal relationship with the *International bibliography of political science* may have ended, but it remains committed to its own unique and indispensable database, the *International political science abstracts*.

Surveys of the discipline, of the kind that we mentioned in chapter 1, arguably provide the most eloquent testimony to the contribution that IPSA has made to international political science. The name of the association may not loom large in indexes to works of these kinds, but the intellectual stature of many of the great scholars whose contributions are acknowledged is likely to have owed much to IPSA. The imprint of IPSA, laid down most visibly in the 1950s and the 1960s, may now be more difficult to detect, but it is none the less potent because of its understated character.

It would, of course, be both unjust and inaccurate to fail to acknowledge the role of other bodies in the promotion of the ideals with which IPSA is associated. In addition to its sister organisations in the social sciences and the humanities, IPSA has shared many of its goals with bodies broader in nature. Indeed, it has enjoyed from the beginning, for reasons that have already been discussed, a particularly warm relationship with Unesco and with the International Social Science Council. But there are also organisation that are narrower in scope, at least geographically: the national political science associations that have played so powerful a role in the creation and sustenance of IPSA. Many of these enjoy a degree of professional organisation that lies far beyond the realistic expectations of IPSA, and administer to the needs of a cohesive community of political scientists that will never resemble IPSA's constituency. Some, such as the American Political Science Association, are themselves international in terms of membership and influence. But IPSA continues to play in international political science the same kind of role as the United Nations plays in international politics: that of a body necessary for the maintenance of inter-regional balance and for ensuring that the voice of the small organism will be heard (at least) alongside that of the large.

This discussion takes us away from the idealistic formulation of Quincy Wright with which we began this chapter. The fact that we can so easily make this transition is itself an eloquent statement: many of the horrors that were part of the consciousness of IPSA's founders have now receded into more distant memory, even if this is assisted from time to time by forms of myopia. The reality is that the prospect of global inter-state conflict has receded, and recent generations of political scientists have focussed on more mundane issues. Not even the most sympathetic history of IPSA could give the association credit for the end of the cold war, but IPSA did consistently manage to show by example, at the *political* level, how the gap between two blocs could be creatively bridged. At the *political science* level, the challenge is less immediate than it was 50 years ago, but if we substitute smaller scale conflicts for the conflagrations of the early twentieth century, the words of IPSA's first president, recalling his impression of a picture from the destroyed Alte Pinakothek in Munich, form an apt summary of a continuing central challenge:

> I was impressed by a striking picture by Tintoretto which depicts Mars seeking to invade the domestic felicity of Venus and Vulcan. Classical mythology recognised some sort of relationship between war on the one hand and love and industry on the other. ... The scientific study of Mars leads to political science, of Venus and Vulcan to the sciences of population and technology. ... If reason can bridle Venus and prevent the increase of the human race ... may not reason also bridle Mars and confine the conflicts, inevitable among the diverse values, cultures and policies of human groups, to methods which will permit the universal society of man to survive, to prosper, and to progress? That is the problem of political science.[2]

---

[2] Ibid, p. 280.

# APPENDICES

## Appendix 1: Members of the IPSA council, 1952-97

### 1a. Representatives of collective members of IPSA

**Africa**
1976: Mohamed Bouzidi, Babatunde Williams
1982: Okwudiba Nnoli
1985: Dani W Nabudere, Okwudiba Nnoli
1988: L Adele Jinadu, Helmy Sharawi
1991: Abdoulahi Bathilly, Peter Anyang Nyong'O
1994: Peter Anyang Nyong'O, Georges Nzongola-Ntalja
1997: L Adele Jinadu, Georges Nzongola-Ntalja

**Argentina**
1958: Segundo V Linares Quintana
1961: Segundo V Linares Quintana
1964: Alberto A Spota
1967: Alberto A Spota
1970: Alfredo Galletti
1973: Alberto Cisneros Lavaller
1982: Alberto Cisneros-Lavaller
1988: Oscar Oszlak
1991: Pablo Kaufer-Barbe, Oscar Oszlak
1994: Arturo Fernandez, Antonio Alberto Spota
1997: Eugenio Kvaternik

**Asia and Pacific**
1985: Carolina G Hernandez

**Australia**
1964: Lloyd G Churchward
1973: J Holmes
1979: Colin Hughes, Preston King
1982: Carole Pateman
1988: Carole Pateman, Marian Simms
1991: Elaine Thompson
1994: Joan Halligan, Marian Simms
1997: Hal Colebatch

*Austria*
1952: Hans Spanner
1985: Eva Kreisky
1988: Anton Pelinka
1991: Ronald Pohoryles

*Belgium (two associations after 1976)*
1952: Maurice P Herremans
1955: Marcel Grégoire
1958: Victor Crabbe
1961: Maurice P Herremans
1964: André Philippart
1967: Léo Moulin
1970: Léo Moulin
1973: Hugo van Hassel
1976: Wilfried Dewachter
1979: Julian Bernard de Clerq, André Philippart
1982: Bernard Crousse, Frank Delmartino
1985: Bernard Crousse, Hugo van Hassel
1988: Frank Delmartino, Yves Frognier
1991: Bernard Crousse, Frank Delmartino
1994: Eric Phillipart
1997: André-Paul Frognier

*Brazil*
1952: Themistocles Cavalcanti
1955: Themistocles Cavalcanti
1958: Georges S Langrod
1961: Themistocles Cavalcanti
1964: Themistocles Cavalcanti
1967: Orlando M Carvalho
1970: Candido Mendes
1973: Candido Mendes
1976: Candido Mendes
1979: Vicente Barreto, Candido Mendes
1982: Carlos H Cardim, Candido Mendes
1985: Candido Mendes
1988: Renato Boschi, Candido Mendes
1991: Candido Mendes, Elisa Reis
1994: Renato Boschi, Candido Mendes
1997: Renato Boschi, Lourdes Sola

*Bulgaria*
1970: Lubomir Dramaliev
1973: Lubomir Dramaliev

1976: Lubomir Dramaliev
1979: Lubomir Dramaliev
1982: Dimiter Dimitrov
1985: Dimiter Dimitrov
1988: Nora Ananieva
1994: Georgi Karasimeonov

*Canada*
1952: CB Macpherson
1955: CB Macpherson
1958: Jacques E Hodgetts, CB Macpherson
1961: Jacques E Hodgetts, Michael K Oliver
1964: Jacques E Hodgetts, CB Macpherson
1967: Jean Laponce, Dale Thomson
1970: Léon Dion, Jean Laponce
1973: Léon Dion, Jean Laponce, John Meisel
1976: Gérard Bergeron, Alan Cairns, John Meisel
1979: John Meisel, Blema Steinberg, André Vachet
1982: Lloyd Brown-John, André Donneur
1985: Caroline Andrew, André Donneur
1988: André Belanger, John C Courtney, André Donneur
1991: Maureen Covell, André Donneur, Peter H Russell
1994: Caroline Andrew, Maureen Covell, Hugh Thorburn
1997: Maureen Covell, OP Dwivedi, Guy Lachapelle

*Ceylon*
1958: IDS Weerawardana

*Chile*
1988: Oscar Godoy

*China*
1982: Bao-Xu Zhao
1985: Bao-Xu Zhao
1988: Chi-An Hu, Yunkun Wang

*Croatia*
1994: Branko Caratan

*Czechoslovakia / Czech Republic*
1973: Miloslav Formanek
1976: Zdenka Ceska
1979: Milan Matous
1982: Josef Blahoz, Milan Matous
1985: Josef Blahoz, Milan Matous
1988: Josef Blahoz, Milan Matous

1994: Jan Škaloud
1997: Jan Škaloud

*Denmark*
1961: Sven Henningsen
1964: Sven Henningsen
1967: Erik Rasmussen
1970: Erik Rasmussen
1973: Ole Pederson
1976: Mogens N Pedersen
1979: Erik Damgaard
1982: Erik Damgaard
1985: Erik Damgaard
1988: Mehdi Mozaffari
1991: Lars Bille
1994: Gunnar Sjöblom
1997: Kurt Klaudi Klausen

*Egypt*
1958: Ahmed El Emary

*Finland*
1952: Lolo Krusius-Ahrenberg
1955: Jan Magnus Jansson, Lolo Krusius-Ahrenberg
1958: Jan Magnus Jansson, Lolo Krusius-Ahrenberg
1961: Risto Hyvarinen, Jan Magnus Jansson
1964: Jan Magnus Jansson, Jaakko Nousiainen
1967: Pertti Pesonen
1970: Ilkka Heiskanen, Pertti Pesonen
1973: Erik Allardt, Sirkka Sinkkonen
1976: Dag Anckar, Göran von Bonsdorff
1979: Pertti Pesonen, Göran von Bonsdorff
1982: Dag Anckar, Ilkka Heiskanen
1985: Dag Anckar, Raimo Väyrynen
1988: Dag Anckar, Tatu Vanhanen
1991: Dag Anckar, Erkki Berndtson
1994: Dag Anckar, Erkki Berndtson
1997: Erkki Berndston, Jan Sundberg

*France*
1952: Raymond Aron, Jacques Chapsal, Maurice Duverger
1955: Jacques Chapsal, Maurice Duverger, Jean Stoetzel
1958: Raymond Aron, Jacques Chapsal, Maurice Duverger
1961: Raymond Aron, Maurice Duverger, Jean Touchard
1964: Jacques Chapsal, Georges Lavau, Jean Stoetzel
1967: Georges Lavau, Jean Stoetzel, Jean Touchard

1970: Alfred Grosser, Georges Lavau, Jean-Louis Quermonne
1973: Alfred Grosser, Jean Leca, Marcel Merle
1976: Jean Charlot, Jean Leca, Marcel Merle
1979: Patrick Gélard, Serge Hurtig, Marcel Merle
1982: Serge Hurtig, Jean Leca, Jean-Luc Parodi
1985: Alain Lancelot, Georges Lavau, Albert Mabileau
1988: Bertrand Badie, Jean Leca, Yves Schemeil
1991: Claude Emeri, Jean Leca, Jean-Luc Parodi
1994: Jean Leca, Jean-Luc Parodi, Jean-Louis Quermonne
1997: Bertrand Badie, Daniel Gaxie, Yves Schemeil

*German Democratic Republic*
1976: Wolfgang Weichelt
1979: Karl-Heinz Roeder
1982: Karl-Heinz Roeder
1985: Karl-Heinz Roeder
1988: Karl-Heinz Roeder

*Germany (Federal Republic)*
1952: Ludwig Bergstraesser
1955: Ludwig Bergstraesser, Otto H von der Gablentz
1958: Gerhard Leibholz, Otto H von der Gablentz
1961: Dolf Sternberger, Otto H von der Gablentz
1964: Dolf Sternberger, Otto H von der Gablentz
1967: Karl Bracher, Kurt Sontheimer
1970: Ernst Otto Czempiel, Kurt Sontheimer, Klaus von Beyme
1973: Wolf-Dieter Narr, Kurt Sontheimer, Klaus von Beyme
1976: Udo Bermach, Klaus von Beyme
1979: Bernd Andresen, Dieter Senghaas, Klaus von Beyme
1982: Michael Th Greven, Dieter Senghaas, Klaus von Beyme
1985: Michael Th Greven, Gerhard Lembruch, Dieter Senghaas
1988: Helga Haftendorn, Gerhard Lembruch, Adrienne Windhoff-Heritier
1991: Gerhard Göhler, Hans-Dieter Klingemann, Adrienne Windhoff-Heritier
1994: Gerhard Göhler, Hans-Dieter Klingemann, Beate Kohler-Koch
1997: Gerhard Göhler, Michael Th Greven, Hans-Dieter Klingemann

*Greece*
1952: Phaidon Vegleris
1955: S Calogeropoulos-Stratis
1958: Phaidon Vegleris
1961: Phaidon Vegleris
1964: Phaidon Vegleris
1976: Phaidon Vegleris
1994: P Nikoforos Diamandorous

*Hungary*
1970: Jozsef Halasz
1985: Györgi Szoboszlai
1988: Kalman Kulcsar
1991: Györgi Szoboszlai
1994: Máté Szábo
1997: Istvan Stumpf

*India*
1952: DN Banerjee
1955: Sadanand V Kogekar
1958: C Joseph Chacko, Sri BM Sharma
1961: C Joseph Chacko, Sadanand V Kogekar
1964: PD Gupta, SAH Haqqi, H Singh
1967: NR Deshpande, SAH Haqqi, H Singh
1970: C Jha, RC Prasad, RN Trivedi
1973: JS Bains, GP Srivastava, RN Trivedi
1976: TC Bose, VK Sukumaran Bose, Nirmal Nair
1979: CA Perumal, LS Rathore, KBY Thotappa
1982: J Ramachandran, LS Rathore, KBY Thotappa
1985: RK Nayak, CA Perumal, LS Rathore
1988: CA Perumal, LS Rathore, KP Singh
1991: CA Perumal, KP Singh, R Thandavan
1994: GK Prasad, DP Singh, KP Singh

*Ireland*
1994: Yvonne Galligan
1997: Yvonne Galligan

*Israel*
1970: Martin Seliger
1973: Martin Seliger
1976: Martin Seliger
1979: Asher Arian, Martin Seliger
1982: Asher Arian, Yitzhak Galnoor
1985: Itzhak Galnoor
1988: Gideon Doron, Itzhak Galnoor
1991: Naomi Chazan, Bernard Susser
1994: Naomi Chazan, Emanuel Gutmann
1997: Naomi Chazan, Gideon Doron

*Italy*
1952: Francesco Vito
1955: Francesco Vito
1958: Mario Viora, Francesco Vito
1961: Mario Viora, Francesco Vito

1964: Mario Viora, Francesco Vito
1967: Mario Viora, Francesco Vito
1970: Giovanni Sartori, Mario Viora
1973: Stefano Passigli, Giovanni Sartori
1976: Stefano Passigli, Giovanni Sartori
1979: Stefano Passigli, Giovanni Sartori
1982: Gianfranco Pasquino, Alberto Spreafico
1988: Luigi Graziano, Leonardo Morlino
1991: Luigi Graziano, Alberto Spreafico
1994: Luigi Graziano, Leonardo Morlino
1997: Mauro Calise, Luigi Graziano

*Japan*
1952: S Nambara
1955: Masamichi Royama
1958: T Imanaka, Kuraji Ogura
1961: H Kinoshita, T Yoshimura
1964: Y Ishii, Kaoru Matsumoto
1967: Norio Ogata, M Saito
1970: Kaoru Matsumoto, E Yokogoshi
1973: Kinhide Mushakoji
1976: Sh Fukushima, Kinhide Mushakoji
1979: Kinhide Mushakoji
1982: Jiro Kamishima, Kinhide Mushakoji
1985: Kinhide Mushakoji, Mitsuru Uchida
1988: Kinhide Mushakoji, Takeshi Sasaki, Mitsuru Uchida
1991: Hiroshi Aruga, Ikuo Kabashima, Takeshi Sasaki
1994: Ikuo Kabashima, Michio Muramatsu, Takeshi Sasaki
1997: Ikuo Kabashima, Michio Muramatsu, Takeshi Sasaki

*Korea (Republic of)*
1970: Young Kook Kim
1973: In-Heung Cheung
1976: D Kim
1979: Hongkoo Lee
1982: Bae-Ho Hahn
1985: Hyung-Sup Yoon
1988: Sung-Joo Han
1991: Sung-Joo Han
1994: Dalchoong Kim
1997: Dalchoong Kim

*Lebanon*
1970: Victor Jabre
1973: Victor Jabre

*Lithuania*
1994: Algis Krupavicius
1997: Algirdas Gricius

*Mexico*
1976: Raul Bejar Navarro
1979: Modesto Seara Vasquez
1982: Rosa Martha Hernandez Portillo
1988: Modesto Seara-Vasques

*Netherlands*
1958: Jan Barents
1970: Hans Daudt
1973: Andries Hoogerwerf
1976: Gerard P Noordzij
1979: Johan K de Vree
1982: Roeland Jaap In't Veld, Ignacio Snellen
1988: Andries Hoogerwerf
1991: Cornelius van der Eijk, MPCM van Schendelen

*Norway*
1958: Stein Rokkan
1961: Stein Rokkan
1964: Stein Rokkan
1967: Stein Rokkan
1970: Stein Rokkan
1973: Stein Rokkan
1976: Stein Kuhnle
1979: Francesco Kjellberg, Stein Kuhnle
1982: Francesco Kjellberg, Bernt Krohn Solvang
1985: Francesco Kjellberg, Stein Kuhnle
1988: Maja Arnestad, William M Lafferty
1991: Jan-Erik Grindheim, William M Lafferty
1994: Dag Ingvar Jacobsen, William M Lafferty
1997: Tore Hansen, William M Lafferty

*Philippines*
1982: Loretta Makasiar Sicat

*Poland*
1955: Stanislaw Ehrlich, Adam Schaff
1958: Stanislaw Ehrlich
1961: Stanislaw Ehrlich
1964: Stanislaw Ehrlich, Jerzy Wiatr
1967: Stanislaw Ehrlich, Jerzy Wiatr
1970: Jerzy Wiatr

1973: Kazimierz Opalek, Jerzy Wiatr
1976: Kazimierz Opalek, Jerzy Wiatr
1979: Kazimierz Opalek, Jerzy Wiatr
1982: Artur Bodnar, Jerzy Wiatr
1985: Czeslaw Mojsiewicz, Longin Pastusiak, Jerzy Wiatr
1988: Czeslaw Mojsiewicz, Longin Pastusiak, Jerzy Wiatr
1991: Czeslaw Mojsiewicz, Longin Pastusiak, Jerzy Wiatr
1994: Czeslaw Mojsiewicz, Krzysztof Palecki, Longin Pastusiak
1997: Andrzej Antoszewski, Marian E Halizak, Krzysztof Palecki

*Romania*
1970: Ioan Ceterchi
1973: Ioan Ceterchi
1976: Ioan Ceterchi
1979: Ioan Ceterchi, Ovidiu Trasnea
1982: Ovidiu Trasnea
1994: Ovidiu Trasnea

*Russia/USSR*
1958: Prof Konstantinov
1961: VS Tadevossian
1967: Viktor Tchikvadze, Vladimir Tumanov, Samuel Zivs
1970: Viktor Tchikvadze, Vladimir Tumanov, Samuel Zivs
1973: Vladimir Tumanov
1976: VO Miller, Georgii Shakhnazarov, Vladimir Tumanov
1979: Vladimir Mshvenieradze, Georgii Shakhnazarov
1982: Vladimir Mshvenieradze, Georgii Shakhnazarov, William Smirnov
1985: Vladimir Mshvenieradze, Georgii Shakhnazarov, William Smirnov
1988: M Maximova, Georgii Shakhnazarov, William Smirnov
1991: Anatoly Dmitriev, Margarita Maximova, William Smirnov
1994: Helen Shestopal, William Smirnov, Valerii Yegorov
1997: Andrei Degtyarev, Anatoly Dmitriev, Helen Shestopal

*Slovak Republic*
1994: Silvia Mihalikova

*Slovenia*
1994: Adolf Bibic
1997: Drago Zajc

*Spain*
1961: Laureano Sanchez-Agesta
1970: Laureano Sanchez Agesta
1979: Julian Santamaria
1982: Julian Santamaria
1997: Carlos R Alba

*Sweden*
1952: Gunnar Heckscher, Nils Stjernquist
1955: Gunnar Heckscher
1958: Gunnar Heckscher, Jörgen Westerståhl
1961: Nils Andrén, Jörgen Westerståhl
1964: Nils Andrén, Jörgen Westerståhl
1967: Per Erik Back, Nils Stjernquist
1970: Olof Ruin, Jörgen Westerståhl
1973: Per Erik Back, Jörgen Westerståhl
1976: Per Erik Back, Olof Ruin
1979: Per Erik Back, Gunnel Gustafsson
1982: Olof Ruin, Jörgen Westerståhl
1985: Kjell Goldmann, Olof Ruin
1988: Axel Hadenius, Olof Ruin
1991: Stefan Björklund, Kjell Goldmann
1997: Christer Jönsson, Jonas Tallberg

*Switzerland*
1961: Jacques Freymond
1964: Jacques Freymond
1970: Dusan Sidjanski
1973: Roy Preiswerk
1976: Daniel Frei
1979: Ernst Bollinger, Daniel Frei
1982: Daniel Frei, Dusan Sidjanski
1988: Pierre Allan, Jean F Freymond
1991: Pierre Allan, Yannis Papadopoulos
1994: Pierre Allan, Jürg Martin Gabriel
1997: Dominique Joye

*Taiwan*
1991: Yung Wei
1994: Tzong-ho Bau
1997: Song Shi Yuan

*Turkey*
1964: Yavuz Abadan
1967: Nermin Abadan
1970: Nermin Abadan
1976: Bahri Sarci
1979: Bahri Sarci
1982: Ergun Özbudun
1988: Ilter Turan
1991: Ergun Özbudun
1997: Ilter Turan

## United Kingdom
1952: D Norman Chester, Albert H Hanson, William A Robson
1955: Peter W Campbell, D Norman Chester, Jack Hayward
1958: D Norman Chester, Wyndraeth H Morris-Jones, William A Robson
1961: D Norman Chester, Samuel E Finer, Wyndraeth H Morris-Jones
1964: D Norman Chester, Harold RG Greaves, Wyndraeth H Morris-Jones
1967: D Norman Chester, Samuel E Finer, Wyndraeth H Morris-Jones
1970: Anthony Birch, D Norman Chester, Samuel E Finer
1973: Anthony Birch, Samuel E Finer, Graeme C Moodie
1976: Anthony Birch, Jack Hayward, Richard Rose
1979: Jack Hayward, Leslie MacFarlane, Richard Rose
1982: Jack Hayward, Margherita Rendel, Richard Rose
1985: Hugh B Berrington, Jack Hayward, Kenneth Newton
1988: Kenneth Newton, Pippa Norris, Philip Norton
1991: Michael Goldsmith, Kenneth Newton, Pippa Norris
1994: Charles Jeffrey, Joni Lovenduski, Ursula Vogel
1997: Wyn Grant, Ian Neary, Ursula Vogel

## USA
1952: R Taylor Cole, Edward H Litchfield, James K Pollock
1955: Evron M Kirkpatrick, James K Pollock
1958: Evron M Kirkpatrick, Benjamin E Lippincott, Charles B Robson
1961: Evron M Kirkpatrick, Harvey C Mansfield, James K Pollock
1964: Carl J Friedrich, Evron M Kirkpatrick, C Herman Pritchett
1967: Merle Fainsod, Carl J Friedrich, Evron M Kirkpatrick
1970: Karl W Deutsch, W Miller, Austin Ranney
1973: Karl W Deutsch, Carl J Friedrich, Samuel P Huntington
1976: James McGregor Burns, Karl W Deutsch, Jeane Kirkpatrick
1979: John Armstrong, Richard L Merritt, William Riker
1982: Philip E Converse, Seymour Martin Lipset, Thomas E Mann
1985: Philip E Converse, Seymour Martin Lipset
1988: Philip E Converse, Seymour Martin Lipset
1991: Harold Jacobson, Theodore J Lowi, Catherine E Rudder
1994: Harold Jacobsen, Catherine E Rudder, Roberta Sigel
1997: Theodore J Lowi, Barbara Nelson, Catherine E Rudder

## Venezuela
1979: Julio Portillo
1982: Miguel Manrique

## Yugoslavia
1952: Jovan Djordjevic, Leon Gerskovic
1955: Jovan Djordjevic, Leon Gerskovic
1958: Jovan Djordjevic, Maks Snuderl
1961: Jovan Djordjevic

1964: Jovan Djordjevic
1967: Jovan Djordjevic, Najdan Pasic
1970: Adolf Bibic, Najdan Pasic
1973: Najdan Pasic
1976: Adolf Bibic, Najdan Pasic
1979: Adolf Bibic, Najdan Pasic
1982: Adolf Bibic, Najdan Pasic
1985: Najdan Pasic, Inge Perko-Separovic
1988: Adolf Bibic, Vojislav Stanovcic
1991: Mijat Damjanovic, Vojislav Stanovcic
1994: Vucina Vasovic
1997: Vukasin Pavlovic

## 1b. *Individual members of IPSA*

*1952*
Jan Barents (Netherlands)
Marcel Bridel (Switzerland)
Fehti Celikbas (Turkey)
Jens Arup Seip (Norway)
Max Sorensen (Denmark)

*1955*
Jan Barents (Netherlands)
Marcel Bridel (Switzerland)

*1958*
Jacques Freymond (Switzerland)

*1967*
Ali Mazrui (Uganda)

*1970*
Ali Mazrui (Uganda)

*1973*
Ilunga Kabongo (Zaire)
Ali Mazrui (Uganda)

*1976*
Vaughan Lewis (Jamaica)
Ali Mazrui (Uganda)

*1979*
Zakaria H Ahmad (Malaysia)
Karl W Deutsch (USA)
Ray Goldstein (New Zealand)
Walter Sanchez (Chile)

**1982**
Karl W Deutsch (USA)
Helga Haftendorn (Germany)
Harold Jackobson (USA)
Jean Laponce (Canada)
John Meisel (Canada)
Richard L Merritt (USA)
Adriano Moaeila (Portugal)
Guillermo O'Donnell (Argentina)
Walter Sanchez (Chile)
Michael Stein (Canada)
Susan Strange (United Kingdom)

**1985**
Nora Ananieva (Bulgaria)
Liliana de Riz (Argentina)
Ray Goldstein (New Zealand)
Carole Pateman (Australia)
Renata Siemenska (Poland)
Elizabeth C Hanson (research committees, USA)
Urs Luterbacher (research committees, Switzerland)
Serge Hurtig (editor, *Abstracts*, France)
Richard L Merritt (editor, book series, USA)
Jean Laponce (editor, *IPSR*, Canada)
John Meisel (editor, *IPSR*, Canada)

**1988**
Likhit Dhiravegin (Thailand)
Perry Mars (Guyana)
Guy Martin (Mali)
Lancine Sylla (Ivory Coast)
Elizabeth C Hanson (research committees, USA)
Harold Jacobson (research committees, USA)
Jan-Erik Lane (research committees, Sweden)
Jacek Tarknowsky (research committees, Poland)
Eileen Wormald (research committees, United Kingdom)
Jean Laponce (editor, *IPSR*, Canada)
John Meisel (editor, *IPSR*, Canada)
Richard L Merritt (editor, book series, USA)

**1991**
Andres Fontana (Argentina)
Carole Pateman (Australia)
Marilyn Hoskin (research committees, USA)
Ulrich Klöti (research committees, Switzerland)

Lawrence Longley (research committees, USA)
Luc Rouban (research committees, France)
Frederick Turner (research committees, USA)
David A Baldwin (study groups, USA)
Najma Chowdhury (study groups, Bangladesh)
Theo Toonen (study groups, Netherlands)
Serge Hurtig (editor, *Abstracts*, France)
Jean Laponce (editor, *IPSR*, Canada)
John Meisel (editor, *IPSR*, Canada)

*1994*
Robert Goodin (Australia)
Peter R Baehr (research committees, Netherlands)
Michael Th Greven (research committees, Germany)
Elizabeth C Hanson (research committees, USA)
RB Jain (research committees, India)
Albert Somit (research committees, USA)
Dhirendra K Vajpey (research committees, USA)
Robert S Walters (research committees, USA)
Arild Underdal (study groups, Norway)
Serge Hurtig (editor, *Abstracts*, France)
Asher Arian (editor, book series, Israel)
Jean Laponce (editor, *IPSR*, Canada)
John Meisel (editor, *IPSR*, Canada)

*1997*
Dirk Berg-Schlosser (research committees, Germany)
Frank Delmartino (research committees, Belgium)
Mattei Dogan (research committees, France)
John Hsieh (research committees, Taiwan)
Henry J Jacek (research committees, Canada)
Lauri Karvonen (research committees, Norway)
Michael Pinto-Duchinsky (research committees, UK)
Hakjoon Kim (study groups, Korea)
Timothy M Shaw (study groups, Canada)
Serge Hurtig (editor, *Abstracts*, France)
Asher Arian (editor, book series, Israel)
Nazli Choucri (editor, *IPSR*, USA)

## Appendix 2: IPSA executive committee members, 1950-2000

### 2a. Listing by executive committee

**Executive committee no. 1 (1950-52)**
| | |
|---|---|
| *President* | Wright, Quincy (University of Chicago, USA) |
| *Vice presidents* | Bridel, Marcel (Université de Lausanne, Switzerland) |
| | Brogan, Denis W (University of Cambridge, UK) |
| *Members* | Barents, Jan (University of Amsterdam, Netherlands) |
| | Celikbas, Fehti (University of Ankara, Turkey) |
| | Duverger, Maurice (Universités de Bordeaux et Paris, France) |
| | Ganon, Isaac (University of Montevideo, Uruguay) |
| | Håstad, Elis (University of Stockholm, Sweden) |
| | Khosla, H (India House, London, UK (India)) |
| | Macpherson, CB (University of Toronto, Canada) |
| | Schaff, Adam (University of Warsaw, Poland) |

**Executive committee no. 2 (1952-55)**
| | |
|---|---|
| *President* | Robson, William A (LSE, London, UK) |
| *Vice presidents* | Duverger, Maurice (Universités de Bordeaux et Paris, France) |
| | Heckscher, Gunnar (University of Stockholm, Sweden) |
| | Pollock, James K (University of Michigan, USA) |
| *Members* | Akzin, Benjamin (Hebrew University, Jerusalem, Israel) |
| | Barents, Jan (University of Amsterdam, Netherlands) |
| | Bridel, Marcel (Université de Lausanne, Switzerland) |
| | Cavalcanti, Themistocles (University of Rio de Janeiro, Brazil) |
| | Chester, D Norman (University of Oxford, UK) |
| | Kogekar, SV (University of Poona, India) |
| | Litchfield, Edward H (University of Pittsburgh, USA) |
| | Macpherson, CB (University of Toronto, Canada) |
| | Vito, Francesco (Catholic University of Milan, Italy) |

**Executive committee no. 3 (1955-58)**
| | |
|---|---|
| *President* | Pollock, James K (University of Michigan, USA) |
| *Past president* | Robson, William A (LSE, London, UK) |
| *Vice presidents* | Akzin, Benjamin (Hebrew University, Jerusalem, Israel) |
| | Chester, D Norman (University of Oxford, UK) |
| | Duverger, Maurice (Université de Paris, France) |
| | Heckscher, Gunnar (University of Stockholm, Sweden) |
| *Members* | Cavalcanti, Themistocles (University of Rio de Janeiro, Brazil) |
| | Djordjevic, Jovan (University of Belgrade, Yugoslavia) |
| | Gablentz, Otto von der (University of Berlin, Germany) |
| | Kogekar, SV (University of Poona, India) |
| | Lange, Oskar (University of Warsaw, Poland) |
| | Litchfield, Edward H (Cornell University, USA) |

Macpherson, CB (University of Toronto, Canada)
Meynaud, Jean (IEP, Paris, France)
Vito, Francesco (Catholic University of Milan, Italy)

**Executive committee no. 4 (1958-61)**

| | |
|---|---|
| *President* | Chapsal, Jacques (IEP, Paris, France) |
| *Past president* | Pollock, James K (University of Michigan, USA) |
| *Vice presidents* | Chachko, C Joseph (University of New Delhi, India) |
| | Chester, D Norman (University of Oxford, UK) |
| | Djordjevic, Jovan (University of Belgrade, Yugoslavia) |
| | Vito, Francesco (Catholic University of Milan, Italy) |
| *Members* | Akzin, Benjamin (Hebrew University, Jerusalem, Israel) |
| | Cavalcanti, Themistocles (University of Rio de Janeiro, Brazil) |
| | Duverger, Maurice (Université de Paris, France) |
| | Ehrlich, Stanislaw (University of Warsaw, Poland) |
| | Freymond, Jacques (Université de Genève, Switzerland) |
| | Gablentz, Otto von der (University of Berlin, Germany) |
| | Jansson, Jan Magnus (University of Helsinki, Finland) |
| | Kirkpatrick, Evron M (APSA, USA) |
| | Robson, William A (LSE, London, UK) |

**Executive committee no. 5 (1961-64)**

| | |
|---|---|
| *President* | Chester, D Norman (University of Oxford, UK) |
| *Past president* | Chapsal, Jacques (IEP, Paris, France) |
| *Vice presidents* | Djordjevic, Jovan (University of Belgrade, Yugoslavia) |
| | Friedrich, Karl J (Harvard University, USA) |
| | Kogekar, SV (University of Poona, India) |
| | Vito, Francesco (University of Milan, Italy) |
| *Members* | Ehrlich, Stanislaw (University of Warsaw, Poland) |
| | Freymond, Jacques (Université de Genève, Switzerland) |
| | Hodgetts, Jacques (University of Toronto, Canada) |
| | Kirkpatrick, Evron M (APSA, USA) |
| | Lavau, Georges (IEP, Paris, France) |
| | Linares Quintana, Segundo V (U. of Buenos Aires, Argentina) |
| | Morris-Jones, Wyndraeth H (University of Durham, UK) |
| | Sternberger, Dolf (University of Heidelberg, Germany) |
| | Tadevossian, VS (Academy of Sciences, Moscow, USSR) |

**Executive committee no. 6 (1964-67)**

| | |
|---|---|
| *President* | Freymond, Jacques (Université de Genève, Switzerland) |
| *Past president* | Chester, D Norman (University of Oxford, UK) |
| *Vice presidents* | Ehrlich, Stanislaw (University of Warsaw, Poland) |
| | Friedrich, Karl J (Harvard University, USA) |
| | Lavau, Georges (Université de Paris, France) |

| | |
|---|---|
| *Members* | Abadan, Yavuz (University of Ankara, Turkey) |
| | Haqqi, SAH (Aligarh Muslim University, India) |
| | Hodgetts, Jacques (University of Toronto, Canada) |
| | Lepechkine, AI (Moscow University, USSR) |
| | Matsumoto, Kaoru (University of Tokyo, Japan) |
| | Morris-Jones, Wyndraeth H (University of Durham, UK) |
| | Philippart, André (University of Brussels, Belgium) |
| | Rokkan, Stein (University of Bergen, Norway) |
| | Spota, Alberto (University of Buenos Aires, Argentina) |
| | Sternberger, Dolf (University of Heidelberg, Germany) |

**Executive committee no. 7 (1967-70)**

| | |
|---|---|
| *President* | Friedrich, Karl J (Harvard University, USA) |
| *Past president* | Freymond, Jacques (Université de Genève, Switzerland) |
| *Vice presidents* | Abadan, Yavuz (University of Ankara, Turkey) |
| | Finer, Samuel E (University of Manchester, UK) |
| | Tchikvadze, Viktor (Academy of Sciences, Moscow, USSR) |
| *Members* | Grosser, Alfred (Université de Paris, France) |
| | Laponce, Jean (University of British Columbia, Canada) |
| | Mazrui, Ali (Makerere University, Kampala, Uganda) |
| | Moulin, Léo (Collège d'Europe, Bruges, Belgium) |
| | Ogata, Norio (University of St. Paul, Japan) |
| | Ranney, Austin (University of Wisconsin, USA) |
| | Rasmussen, Erik (University of Aarhus, Denmark) |
| | Sontheimer, Kurt (Free University of Berlin, Germany) |
| | Viora, Mario (University of Torino, Italy) |
| | Wiatr, Jerzy (University of Warsaw, Poland) |

**Executive committee no. 8 (1970-73)**

| | |
|---|---|
| *President* | Rokkan, Stein (University of Bergen, Norway) |
| *Past president* | Friedrich, Karl J (Harvard University, USA) |
| *Vice presidents* | Deutsch, Karl (Harvard University, USA) |
| | Grosser, Alfred (IEP, Paris, France) |
| | Mazrui, Ali (Makerere University, Kampala, Uganda) |
| | Tchikvadze, Viktor (Academy of Sciences, Moscow, USSR) |
| *Members* | Aridi, Béchir (University of Lebanon, Lebanon) |
| | Finer, Samuel E (University of Manchester, UK) |
| | Laponce, Jean (University of British Columbia, Canada) |
| | Mendès, Candido (Univ. de Pesquisas de Rio de Janeiro, Brazil) |
| | Moulin, Léo (Collège d'Europe, Bruges, Belgium) |
| | Pasic, Najdan (University of Belgrade, Yugoslavia) |
| | Sartori, Giovanni (University of Florence, Italy) |
| | Seliger, Martin (Hebrew University, Jerusalem, Israel) |
| | Sontheimer, Kurt (Free University of Berlin, Germany) |

Trivedi, RN (Ranchi University, India)
Westerståhl, Jörgen (University of Göteborg, Sweden)
Wiatr, Jerzy (University of Warsaw, Poland)

*Executive committee no. 9 (1973-76)*

| | |
|---|---|
| *President* | Laponce, Jean (University of British Columbia, Canada) |
| *Past president* | Rokkan, Stein (University of Bergen, Norway) |
| *Vice presidents* | Beyme, Klaus von (University of Heidelberg, Germany) |
| | Deutsch, Karl (Harvard University, USA) |
| | Mendès, Candido (Univ. de Pesquisas de Rio de Janeiro, Brazil) |
| | Tumanov, Vladimir (Soviet PSA, Moscow, USSR) |
| *Members* | Birch, Anthony (University of Exeter, UK) |
| | Ceterchi, Ioan (Romanian PSA, Romania) |
| | Mazrui, Ali (Makerere University, Kampala, Uganda) |
| | Meisel, John (Queen's University, Kingston, Canada) |
| | Merle, Marcel (Université de Paris, France) |
| | Mushakoji, Kinhide (Sophia University, Tokyo, Japan) |
| | Opalek, Kazimierz (University of Warsaw, Poland) |
| | Pasic, Najdan (University of Belgrade, Yugoslavia) |
| | Sartori, Giovanni (University of Florence, Italy) |
| | Seliger, Martin (Hebrew University, Jerusalem, Israel) |
| | Sinkkonen, Sirkka (University of Helsinki, Finland) |
| | Trivedi, RN (Ranchi University, India) |

*Executive committee no. 10 (1976-79)*

| | |
|---|---|
| *President* | Deutsch, Karl (Harvard University, USA) |
| *Past president* | Laponce, Jean (University of British Columbia, Canada) |
| *First vice president* | Mendès, Candido (Univ. de Pesquisas de Rio de Janeiro, Brazil) |
| *Vice presidents* | Beyme, Klaus von (University of Heidelberg, Germany) |
| | Birch, Anthony (University of Exeter, UK) |
| | Merle, Marcel (Université de Paris, France) |
| | Shakhnazarov, Georgii (Soviet PSA, Moscow, USSR) |
| *Members* | Bibic, Adolf (University of Ljubljana, Yugoslavia) |
| | Bose, Nirmal (University of Calcutta, India) |
| | Bouzidi, Mohamed (University of Rabat, Morocco) |
| | Ceterchi, Ioan (University of Bucharest, Romania) |
| | Frei, Daniel (University of Zurich, Switzerland) |
| | Mushakoji, Kinhide (Sophia University, Tokyo, Japan) |
| | Opalek, Kazimierz (University of Warsaw, Poland) |
| | Passigli, Stefano (University of Florence, Italy) |
| | Pedersen, Mogens (University of Odense, Denmark) |
| | Seliger, Martin (Hebrew University, Jerusalem, Israel) |
| | Williams, Babatunde (University of Lagos, Nigeria) |

*Executive committee no. 11 (1979-82)*

*President*               Mendès, Candido (Univ. de Pesquisas de Rio de Janeiro, Brazil)
*Past president*          Deutsch, Karl (Harvard University, USA)
*First vice president*    Shakhnazarov, Georgii (Soviet PSA, Moscow, USSR)
*Vice presidents*         Frei, Daniel (University of Zurich, Switzerland)
                          Hurtig, Serge (FNSP, Paris, France)
                          Merritt, Richard (University of Illinois, USA)
                          Mushakoji, Kinhide (Sophia University, Tokyo, Japan)
                          Wiatr, Jerzy (University of Warsaw, Poland)
*Members*                 Arian, Asher (University of Tel Aviv, Israel)
                          Bibic, Adolf (University of Ljubljana, Yugoslavia)
                          Hayward, Jack (University of Hull, UK)
                          Kjellberg, Francesco (University of Oslo, Norway)
                          Meisel, John (Queen's Univ, Kingston, Canada)
                          Özbudun, Ergun (University of Ankara, Turkey)
                          Passigli, Stefano (University of Florence, Italy)
                          Perumal, CA (University of Madras, India)
                          Portillo, Julio (University of Caracas, Venezuela)
                          Senghaas, Dieter (University of Bremen, Germany)

*Executive committee no. 12 (1982-85)*

*President*               Beyme, Klaus von (University of Heidelberg, Germany)
*Past president*          Mendès, Candido (Univ. de Pesquisas de Rio de Janeiro, Brazil)
*First vice president*    Shakhnazarov, Georgii (Soviet PSA, Moscow, USSR)
*Vice presidents*         Hurtig, Serge (FNSP, Paris, France)
                          Lipset, Seymour Martin (Stanford University, USA)
                          Mushakoji, Kinhide (Sophia University, Tokyo, Japan)
                          O'Donnell, Guillermo (IUPERJ, Rio de Janeiro, Brazil)
*Members*                 Arian, Asher (University of Tel Aviv, Israel)
                          DeVree, Johan (University of Amsterdam, Netherlands)
                          Hayward, Jack (University of Hull, UK)
                          Nnoli, Okwudiba (University of Nsukka, Nigeria)
                          Özbudun, Ergun (University of Ankara, Turkey)
                          Perko-Separovic, Inge (University of Zagreb, Yugoslavia)
                          Rathore, LS (University of Jodphur, India)
                          Ruin, Olof (University of Stockholm, Sweden)
                          Santamaria, Julian (University of Santiago, Spain)
                          Senghaas, Dieter (University of Bremen, Germany)
                          Spreafico, Alberto (University of Firenze, Italy)

*Executive committee no. 13 (1985-88)*

*President*               Mushakoji, Kinhide (Sophia University, Tokyo, Japan)
*Past president*          Beyme, Klaus von (University of Heidelberg, Germany)

| Vice presidents | Lavau, Georges (IEP, Paris, France) |
| --- | --- |
| | Lipset, Seymour Martin (Stanford University, USA) |
| | Nabudere, Dani W (University of Helsingor, Denmark) |
| | O'Donnell, Guillermo (IUPERJ, Rio de Janeiro, Brazil) |
| | Shakhnazarov, Georgii (Soviet PSA, Moscow, USSR) |
| Members | DeVree, Johan (University of Utrecht, Netherlands) |
| | Donneur, André (Université de Montréal, Canada) |
| | Galnoor, Itzhak (Hebrew University, Jerusalem, Israel) |
| | Lee, Hongkoo (Seoul National University, Korea) |
| | Lehmbruch, Gerhard (University of Konstanz, Germany) |
| | Newton, Kenneth (University of Dundee, UK) |
| | Perko-Separovic, Inge (University of Zagreb, Yugoslavia) |
| | Röder, Karl-Heinz (Acad. of Sciences, Berlin, German DR) |
| | Ruin, Olof (University of Stockholm, Sweden) |
| | Spreafico, Alberto (University of Firenze, Italy) |
| | Zhao, Bao-Xu (Peking University, China) |

*Executive committee no. 14 (1988-91)*

| President | O'Donnell, Guillermo (CEBRAP, Sao Paulo, Brazil) |
| --- | --- |
| Past president | Mushakoji, Kinhide (United Nations University, Tokyo, Japan) |
| First vice president | Pateman, Carole (University of Sydney, Australia) |
| Vice presidents | Hu, Chi-An (Peking University, China) |
| | Jacobson, Harold (University of Michigan, USA) |
| | Lehmbruch, Gerhard (University of Konstanz, Germany) |
| | Smirnov, William (Academy of Sciences, Moscow, USSR) |
| Members | Allan, Pierre (Université de Genève, Switzerland) |
| | Anckar, Dag (Åbo Academi, Åbo, Finland) |
| | Donneur, André (Université de Québec, Montréal, Canada) |
| | Galnoor, Itzhak (Hebrew University, Jerusalem, Israel) |
| | Han, Sung-Joo (Korea University, Seoul, Korea) |
| | Leca, Jean (IEP, Paris, France) |
| | Morlino, Leonardo (University of Florence, Italy) |
| | Newton, Kenneth (University of Dundee, UK) |
| | Pastusiak, Longin (Polish Inst. of Int. Affairs, Warsaw, Poland) |
| | Reis, Elisa (IUPERJ, Rio de Janeiro, Brazil) |
| | Röder, Karl-Heinz (Acad. of Sciences, Berlin, German DR) |

*Executive committee no. 15 (1991-94)*

| President | Pateman, Carole (University of California, Los Angeles, USA) |
| --- | --- |
| Past president | O'Donnell, Guillermo (CEBRAP, Sao Paulo, Brazil) |
| First vice president | Leca, Jean (IEP, Paris, France) |
| Vice presidents | Chazan, Naomi (Hebrew University, Jerusalem, Israel) |
| | Han, Sung-Joo (Korea University, Seoul, Korea) |

Lowi, Theodore J (Cornell University, USA)
Pastusiak, Longin (Polish Inst. of Int. Affairs, Warsaw, Poland)
*Members*      Allan, Pierre (Université de Genève, Switzerland)
Anckar, Dag (Åbo Academi, Åbo, Finland)
Anyang' Nyong'o, Peter (AAPS, Kenya)
Covell, Maureen (Simon Fraser University, Canada)
Graziano, Luigi (University of Torino, Italy)
Klingemann, Hans-Dieter (WZB, Berlin, Germany)
Norris, Pippa (University of Edinburgh, UK)
Oszlak, Oscar (CEDES, Buenos Aires, Argentina)
Reis, Elisa (IUPERJ, Rio de Janeiro, Brazil)
Sasaki, Takeshi (University of Tokyo, Japan)
Smirnov, William (Academy of Sciences, Moscow, USSR)

*Executive committee no. 16 (1994-97)*
*President*            Leca, Jean (IEP, Paris, France)
*Past president*       Pateman, Carole (University of California, Los Angeles, USA)
*First vice president* Lowi, Theodore J (Cornell University, USA)
*Vice presidents*      Chazan, Naomi (Hebrew University, Jerusalem, Israel)
Graziano, Luigi (University of Torino, Italy)
Kim, Dalchoong (Yonsei University, Seoul, Korea)
Klingemann, Hans-Dieter (WZB, Berlin, Germany)
*Members*              Boschi, Renato (IUPERJ, Rio de Janeiro, Brazil)
Covell, Maureen (Simon Fraser University, Canada)
Lafferty, William (University of Oslo, Norway)
Nzongola-Ntalaja, Georges (AAPS, Zimbabwe)
Palecki, Krzysztof (Jagiellonian University, Krakow, Poland)
Sasaki, Takeshi (University of Tokyo, Japan)
Shestopal, Helen (University of Moscow University, Russia)
Singh, DP (University of Madras, India)
Sjöblom, Gunnar (University of Copenhagen, Denmark)
Škaloud, Jan (Prague University of Economics, Czech Republic)
Vogel, Ursula (University of Manchester, UK)

*Executive committee no. 17 (1997-2000)*
*President*            Lowi, Theodore J (Cornell University, USA)
*Past president*       Leca, Jean (IEP, Paris, France)
*First vice president* Kim, Dalchoong (Yonsei University, Seoul, Korea)
*Vice presidents*      Boschi, Renato (IUPERJ, Rio de Janeiro, Brazil)
Palecki, Krzysztof (Jagiellonian University, Krakow, Poland)
Shestopal, Helen (Moscow University, Russia)
Sjöblom, Gunnar (University of Copenhagen, Denmark)
Vogel, Ursula (University of Manchester, UK)

*Members*     Alba, Carlos R (Universidad Autónoma de Madrid, Spain)
Calise, Mauro (University of Naples, Italy)
Doron, Gideon (Tel Aviv University, Israel)
Jinadu, L Adele (Lagos State University, Nigeria)
Kaase, Max (Wissenschaftszentrum, Berlin, Germany)
Kabashima, Ikuo (University of Tokyo, Japan)
Lachapelle, Guy (Université Concordia, Canada)
McClain, Paula D (University of Virginia, USA)
Schemeil, Yves (IEP, Grenoble, France)
Škaloud, Jan (Prague University of Economics, Czech Republic)

## 2b Listing in alphabetical order

Abadan, Yavuz (University of Ankara, Turkey) — member (1964-67); vice president (1967-70)

Akzin, Benjamin (Hebrew University, Jerusalem, Israel) — member (1952-55); vice president (1955-58); member (1958-61)

Alba, Carlos R (Universidad Autónoma de Madrid, Spain) — member (1997-2000)

Allan, Pierre (Université de Genève, Switzerland) — member (1988-91, 1991-94)

Anckar, Dag (Åbo Academi, Åbo, Finland) — member (1988-91, 1991-94)

Anyang' Nyong'o, Peter (AAPS, Kenya) — member (1991-94)

Arian, Asher (University of Tel Aviv, Israel) — member (1979-82, 1982-85)

Aridi, Béchir (University of Lebanon, Lebanon) — member (1970-73)

Barents, Jan (University of Amsterdam, Netherlands) — member (1950-52, 1952-55)

Beyme, Klaus von (University of Heidelberg, Germany) — vice president (1973-76, 1976-79); president (1982-85); past president (1985-88)

Bibic, Adolf (University of Ljubljana, Yugoslavia) — member (1976-79, 1979-82)

Birch, Anthony (University of Exeter, UK) — member (1973-76); vice president (1976-79)

Boschi, Renato (IUPERJ, Rio de Janeiro, Brazil) — member (1994-97); vice president (1997-2000)

Bose, Nirmal (University of Calcutta, India) — member (1976-79)

Bouzidi, Mohamed (University of Rabat, Morocco) — member (1976-79)

Bridel, Marcel (Université de Lausanne, Switzerland) — vice president (1950-52); member (1952-55)

Brogan, Denis W (University of Cambridge, UK) — vice president (1950-52)

Calise, Mauro (University of Naples, Italy) — member (1997-2000)

Cavalcanti, Themistocles (University of Rio de Janeiro, Brazil) — member (1952-55, 1955-58, 1958-61)

Celikbas, Fehti (University of Ankara, Turkey) — member (1950-52)

Ceterchi, Ioan (Romanian Political Science Association, Romania) — member (1973-76, 1976-79)

Chachko, C Joseph (University of New Delhi, India) – vice president (1958-61)

Chapsal, Jacques (IEP, Paris, France) – president (1958-61); past president (1961-64)

Chazan, Naomi (Hebrew University, Jerusalem, Israel) – vice president (1991-94, 1994-97)

Chester, D Norman (University of Oxford, UK) – member (1952-55); vice president (1955-58, 1958-61); president (1961-64); past president (1964-67)

Covell, Maureen (Simon Fraser University, Canada) – member (1991-94, 1994-97)

Deutsch, Karl (Harvard University, USA) – vice president (1970-73, 1973-76); president (1976-79); past president (1979-82)

DeVree, Johan (University of Amsterdam, Netherlands) – member (1982-85, 1985-88)

Djordjevic, Jovan (University of Belgrade, Yugoslavia) – member (1955-58); vice president (1958-61, 1961-64)

Donneur, André (Université de Montréal, Canada) – member (1985-88, 1988-91)

Doron, Gideon (Tel Aviv University, Israel) – member (1997-2000)

Duverger, Maurice (Universités de Bordeaux et Paris, France) – member (1950-52); vice president (1952-55, 1955-58); member (1958-61)

Ehrlich, Stanislaw (University of Warsaw, Poland) – member (1958-61, 1961-64); vice president (1964-67)

Finer, Samuel E (University of Manchester, UK) – vice president (1967-70); member (1970-73)

Frei, Daniel (University of Zurich, Switzerland) – member (1976-79); vice president (1979-82)

Freymond, Jacques (Université de Genève, Switzerland) – member (1958-61, 1961-64); president (1964-67); past president (1967-70)

Friedrich, Karl J (Harvard University, USA) – vice president (1961-64, 1964-67); president (1967-70); past president (1970-73)

Gablentz, Otto von der (University of Berlin, Germany) – member (1955-58, 1958-61)

Galnoor, Itzhak (Hebrew University, Jerusalem, Israel) – member (1985-88, 1988-91)

Ganon, Isaac (University of Montevideo, Uruguay) – member (1950-52)

Graziano, Luigi (University of Torino, Italy) – member (1991-94); vice president (1994-97)

Grosser, Alfred (Université de Paris, France) – member (1967-70); vice president (1970-73)

Han, Sung-Joo (Korea University, Seoul, Korea) – member (1988-91); vice president (1991-94)

Haqqi, SAH (Aligarh Muslim University, India) – member (1964-67)

Håstad, Elis (University of Stockholm, Sweden) – member (1950-52)

Hayward, Jack (University of Hull, UK) – member (1979-82, 1982-85)

Heckscher, Gunnar (University of Stockholm, Sweden) — vice president (1952-55, 1955-58)

Hodgetts, Jacques (University of Toronto, Canada) — member (1961-64, 1964-67)

Hu, Chi-An (Peking University, China) — vice president (1988-91)

Hurtig, Serge (FNSP, Paris, France) — vice president (1979-82, 1982-85)

Jacobson, Harold (University of Michigan, USA) — vice president (1988-91)

Jansson, Jan Magnus (University of Helsinki, Finland) — member (1958-61)

Jinadu, L Adele (Lagos State University, Nigeria) — member (1997-2000)

Kaase, Max (Wissenschaftszentrum, Berlin, Germany) — member (1997-2000)

Kabashima, Ikuo (University of Tokyo, Japan) — member (1997-2000)

Khosla, H (India House, London, UK (India)) — member (1950-52)

Kim, Dalchoong (Yonsei University, Seoul, Korea) — vice president (1994-97); first vice president (1997-2000)

Kirkpatrick, Evron M (APSA, USA) — member (1958-61, 1961-64)

Kjellberg, Francesco (University of Oslo, Norway) — member (1979-82)

Klingemann, Hans-Dieter (Wissenschaftszentrum, Berlin, Germany) — member (1991-94); vice president (1994-97)

Kogekar, SV (University of Poona, India) — member (1952-55, 1955-58); vice president (1961-64)

Lachapelle, Guy (Université Concordia, Canada) — member (1997-2000)

Lafferty, William (University of Oslo, Norway) — member (1994-97)

Lange, Oskar (University of Warsaw, Poland) — member (1955-58)

Laponce, Jean (University of British Columbia, Canada) — member (1967-70, 1970-73); president (1973-76); past president (1976-79)

Lavau, Georges (IEP, Paris, France) — member (1961-64); vice president (1964-67, 1985-88)

Leca, Jean (IEP, Paris, France) — member (1988-91); first vice president (1991-94); president (1994-97); past president (1997-2000)

Lee, Hongkoo (Seoul National University, Korea) — member (1985-88)

Lehmbruch, Gerhard (University of Konstanz, Germany) — member (1985-88); vice president (1988-91)

Lepechkine, AI (Moscow University, USSR) — member (1964-67)

Linares Quintana, Segundo V (University of Buenos Aires, Argentina) — member (1961-64)

Lipset, Seymour Martin (Stanford University, USA) — vice president (1982-85, 1985-88)

Litchfield, Edward H (University of Pittsburgh, USA) — member (1952-55, 1955-58)

Lowi, Theodore J (Cornell University, USA) — vice president (1991-94); first vice president (1994-97); president (1997-2000)

Macpherson, CB (University of Toronto, Canada) — member (1950-52, 1952-55, 1955-58)

Matsumoto, Kaoru (University of Tokyo, Japan) — member (1964-67)

Mazrui, Ali (Makerere University, Kampala, Uganda) — member (1967-70); vice president (1970-73); member (1973-76)

McClain, Paula D (University of Virginia, USA) — member (1997-2000)

Meisel, John (Queen's University, Kingston, Canada) — member (1973-76, 1979-82)

Mendès, Candido (Universitad de Pesquisas de Rio de Janeiro, Brazil) — member (1970-73); vice president (1973-76); first vice president (1976-79); president (1979-82); past president (1982-85)

Merle, Marcel (Université de Paris, France) — member (1973-76); vice president (1976-79)

Merritt, Richard (University of Illinois, USA) — vice president (1979-82)

Meynaud, Jean (IEP, Paris, France) — member (1955-58)

Morlino, Leonardo (University of Florence, Italy) — member (1988-91)

Morris-Jones, Wyndraeth H (University of Durham, UK) — member (1961-64, 1964-67)

Moulin, Léo (Collège d'Europe, Bruges, Belgium) — member (1967-70, 1970-73)

Mushakoji, Kinhide (Sophia University, Tokyo, Japan) — member (1973-76, 1976-79); vice president (1979-82, 1982-85); president (1985-88); past president (1988-91)

Nabudere, Dani W (University of Helsingor, Denmark) — vice president (1985-88)

Newton, Kenneth (University of Dundee, UK) — member (1985-88, 1988-91)

Nnoli, Okwudiba (University of Nsukka, Nigeria) — member (1982-85)

Norris, Pippa (University of Edinburgh, UK) — member (1991-94)

Nzongola-Ntalaja, Georges (AAPS, Zimbabwe) — member (1994-97)

O'Donnell, Guillermo (IUPERJ, Rio de Janeiro, Brazil) — vice president (1982-85, 1985-88); president (1988-91); past president (1991-94)

Ogata, Norio (University of St. Paul, Japan) — member (1967-70)

Opalek, Kazimierz (University of Warsaw, Poland) — member (1973-76, 1976-79)

Oszlak, Oscar (CEDES, Buenos Aires, Argentina) — member (1991-94)

Özbudun, Ergun (University of Ankara, Turkey) — member (1979-82, 1982-85)

Palecki, Krzysztof (Jagiellonian University, Krakow, Poland) — member (1994-97); vice president (1997-2000)

Pasic, Najdan (University of Belgrade, Yugoslavia) — member (1970-73, 1973-76)

Passigli, Stefano (University of Florence, Italy) — member (1976-79, 1979-82)

Pastusiak, Longin (Polish Institute of International Affairs, Warsaw, Poland) — member (1988-91); vice president (1991-94)

Pateman, Carole (University of Sydney, Australia) — first vice president (1988-91); president (1991-94); past president (1994-97)

Pedersen, Mogens (University of Odense, Denmark) — member (1976-79)

Perko-Separovic, Inge (University of Zagreb, Yugoslavia) — member (1982-85, 1985-88)

Perumal, CA (University of Madras, India) — member (1979-82)

Philippart, André (University of Brussels, Belgium) — member (1964-67)

Pollock, James K (University of Michigan, USA) — vice president (1952-55); president (1955-58); past president (1958-61)

Portillo, Julio (University of Caracas, Venezuela) — member (1979-82)

Ranney, Austin (University of Wisconsin, USA) — member (1967-70)

Rasmussen, Erik (University of Aarhus, Denmark) — member (1967-70)

Rathore, LS (University of Jodphur, India) — member (1982-85)

Reis, Elisa (IUPERJ, Rio de Janeiro, Brazil) — member (1988-91, 1991-94)

Robson, William A (LSE, London, UK) — president (1952-55); past president (1955-58); member (1958-61)

Röder, Karl-Heinz (Academy of Sciences, Berlin, German Democratic Republic) — member (1985-88, 1988-91)

Rokkan, Stein (University of Bergen, Norway) — member (1964-67); president (1970-73); past president (1973-76)

Ruin, Olof (University of Stockholm, Sweden) — member (1982-85, 1985-88)

Santamaria, Julian (University of Santiago, Spain) — member (1982-85)

Sartori, Giovanni (University of Florence, Italy) — member (1970-73, 1973-76)

Sasaki, Takeshi (University of Tokyo, Japan) — member (1991-94, 1994-97)

Schaff, Adam (University of Warsaw, Poland) — member (1950-52)

Schemeil, Yves (IEP, Grenoble, France) — member (1997-2000)

Seliger, Martin (Hebrew University, Jerusalem, Israel) — member (1970-73, 1973-76, 1976-79)

Senghaas, Dieter (University of Bremen, Germany) — member (1979-82, 1982-85)

Shakhnazarov, Georgii (Soviet Political Science Association, Moscow, USSR) — vice president (1976-79); first vice president (1979-82, 1982-85); vice president (1985-88)

Shestopal, Helen (University of Moscow University, Russia) — member (1994-97); vice president (1997-2000)

Singh, DP (University of Madras, India) — member (1994-97)

Sinkkonen, Sirkka (University of Helsinki, Finland) — member (1973-76)

Sjöblom, Gunnar (University of Copenhagen, Denmark) — member (1994-97); vice president (1997-2000)

Škaloud, Jan (Prague University of Economics, Czech Republic) — member (1994-97, 1997-2000)

Smirnov, William (Academy of Sciences, Moscow, USSR) — vice president (1988-91); member (1991-94)

Sontheimer, Kurt (Free University of Berlin, Germany) — member (1967-70, 1970-73)

Spota, Alberto (University of Buenos Aires, Argentina) — member (1964-67)

Spreafico, Alberto (University of Firenze, Italy) — member (1982-85, 1985-88)

Sternberger, Dolf (University of Heidelberg, Germany) – member (1961-64, 1964-67)

Tadevossian, VS (Academy of Sciences, Moscow, USSR) – member (1961-64)

Tchikvadze, Viktor (Academy of Sciences, Moscow, USSR) – vice president (1967-70, 1970-73)

Trivedi, RN (Ranchi University, India) – member (1970-73, 1973-76)

Tumanov, Vladimir (Soviet Political Science Association, Moscow, USSR) – vice president (1973-76)

Viora, Mario (University of Torino, Italy) – member (1967-70)

Vito, Francesco (Catholic University of Milan, Italy) – member (1952-55, 1955-58); vice president (1958-61, 1961-64)

Vogel, Ursula (University of Manchester, UK) – member (1994-97); vice president (1997-2000)

Westerståhl, Jörgen (University of Göteborg, Sweden) – member (1970-73)

Wiatr, Jerzy (University of Warsaw, Poland) – member (1967-70, 1970-73); vice president (1979-82)

Williams, Babatunde (University of Lagos, Nigeria) – member (1976-79)

Wright, Quincy (University of Chicago, USA) – president (1950-52)

Zhao, Bao-Xu (Peking University, China) – member (1985-88)

## Appendix 3: Executive committee meetings 1950-2000

| 1. | 1950 | Sep 4-9 | Zurich |
|---|---|---|---|
| 2. | 1951 | May 28-29 | Lausanne |
| 3. | 1952 | Sep 7-9 | Hague |

| 4. | 1952 | Sep 12 | Hague |
|---|---|---|---|
| 5. | 1953 | Jun 8-9 | Paris |
| 6. | 1954 | Apr 5-10 | Florence |
| 7. | 1955 | Aug 19 | Stockholm |

| 8. | 1955 | Aug 27-28 | Stockholm |
|---|---|---|---|
| 9. | 1956 | Sep 8-9 | La Tour-de-Peilz |
| 10. | 1957 | Sep 8-9 | Pittsburgh |
| 11. | 1958 | Sep 14 | Rome |

| 12. | 1958 | Sep 20-21 | Rome |
|---|---|---|---|
| 13. | 1959 | Aug 30-31 | Opatija |
| 14. | 1960 | Sep 11-13, 16 | Ann Arbor |
| 15. | 1961 | Sep 24 | Paris |

| 16. | 1961 | Sep 30 | Paris |
|---|---|---|---|
| 17. | 1962 | Sep 10, 13 | Freudenstadt |
| 18. | 1963 | Sep 18, 21 | Oxford |
| 19. | 1964 | Sep 20 | Geneva |

| 20. | 1964 | Sep 26 | Geneva |
|---|---|---|---|
| 21. | 1965 | Sep 13, 17 | Grenoble |
| 22. | 1966 | Sep 18 | Jablonna |
| 23. | 1967 | Sep 16 | Brussels |

| 24. | 1967 | Sep 23 | Brussels |
|---|---|---|---|
| 25. | 1968 | Sep 15 | Salzburg |
| 26. | 1969 | Sep 9, 13 | Turin |
| 27. | 1970 | Aug 30 | Munich |

| 28. | 1970 | Sep 5 or 6 | Munich |
|---|---|---|---|
| 29. | 1971 | Sep 14 | Louvain |
| 30. | 1972 | Sep 14 | Bucharest |
| 31. | 1973 | Aug 18 or 19 | Montreal |

| 32. | 1973 | Aug 25 | Montreal |
|---|---|---|---|
| 33. | 1974 | Sep 11 | Jerusalem |
| 34. | 1975 | Sep 11 | Dubrovnik |
| 35. | 1976 | Aug 15 | Edinburgh |

| 36. | 1976 | Aug 21 | Edinburgh |
|---|---|---|---|
| 37. | 1977 | Aug 31 | Cracow |
| 38. | 1978 | Aug 23, 24, 26 | Rio de Janeiro |

| 39. | 1979 | Aug 12 | Moscow |
|-----|------|--------|--------|
| 40. | 1979 | Aug 18 | Moscow |
| 41. | 1980 | Jan 9 | Paris |
| 42. | 1981 | Jan 6-7 | Zurich |
| 43. | 1982 | Mar 27-28 | Tokyo |
| 44. | 1982 | Aug 8 | Rio de Janeiro |
| 45. | 1982 | Aug 14 | Rio de Janeiro |
| 46. | 1983 | Jan 8 | West Berlin |
| 47. | 1983 | Sep 5 | Urbana-Champaign |
| 48. | 1984 | Apr 5 | Florence |
| 49. | 1985 | Mar 14 | Zagreb |
| 50. | 1985 | Jul 14 | Paris |
| 51. | 1985 | Jul 20 | Paris |
| 52. | 1986 | Mar 8-10 | Buenos Aires |
| 53. | 1986 | Sep 30-Oct 2 | Ottawa |
| 54. | 1987 | Apr 4-5 | Berlin, GDR |
| 55. | 1988 | Mar 21-22 | Moscow |
| 56. | 1988 | Aug 27 | Washington |
| 57. | 1988 | Sep 2 | Washington |
| 58. | 1989 | Apr 10-11 | Paris |
| 59. | 1989 | Aug 22-23 | Oslo |
| 60. | 1990 | May 25-26 | Seoul |
| 61. | 1991 | Apr 21 | Warsaw |
| 62. | 1991 | Jul 20 | Buenos Aires |
| 63. | 1991 | Jul 26 | Buenos Aires |
| 64. | 1992 | Jan 30-31 | Madras |
| 65. | 1992 | Sep 1 | Chicago |
| 66. | 1993 | Apr 19-20 | Leicester |
| 67. | 1994 | Mar 23-24 | Kyoto |
| 68. | 1994 | Aug 20 | Berlin |
| 69. | 1994 | Aug 26 | Berlin |
| 70. | 1995 | Jan 11-12 | Taipei |
| 71. | 1995 | Aug 26-27 | Prague |
| 72. | 1996 | Apr 24-25 | Oslo |
| 73. | 1997 | Mar 6-8 | Rio de Janeiro |
| 74. | 1997 | Aug 16 | Seoul |
| 75. | 1997 | Aug 22 | Seoul |
| 76. | 1998 | Feb 14-15 | Quebec |
| 77. | 1998 | Sep 1-2 | Boston |
| 78. | 1999 | Apr 25-26 | Krakow |
| 79. | 1999 | Oct 6 | Naples |
| 80. | 2000 | Feb 27 | Jerusalem |

## Appendix 4: IPSA Revenue and expenditure, 1955-98

| Year | Revenue | Expenditure | Balance |
|------|---------|-------------|---------|
| 1955 | 23,273 | 22,883 | 390 |
| 1956 | 19,705 | 13,732 | 5,973 |
| 1957 | 38,435 | 38,717 | -282 |
| 1958 | 38,972 | 40,573 | -1,601 |
| 1959 | 37,509 | 38,572 | -1,063 |
| 1960 | 30,197 | 22,247 | 7,950 |
| 1961 | 39,070 | 37,730 | 1,340 |
| 1962 | 16,610 | 17,730 | -1,120 |
| 1963 | 18,650 | 17,650 | 1,000 |
| 1964 | 61,134 | 66,220 | -5,086 |
| 1965 | 27,436 | 28,452 | -1,016 |
| 1966 | 29,631 | 31,677 | -2,046 |
| 1967 | 85,670 | 75,198 | 10,472 |
| 1968 | 35,052 | 31,495 | 3,557 |
| 1969 | 73,109 | 63,183 | 9,926 |
| 1970 | 109,065 | 105,864 | 3,201 |
| 1971 | 40,320 | 41,251 | -931 |
| 1972 | 43,178 | 49,937 | -6,759 |
| 1973 | 145,839 | 150,274 | -4,435 |
| 1974 | 44,031 | 49,660 | -5,629 |
| 1975 | 118,329 | 119,738 | -1,409 |
| 1976 | 114,767 | 106,612 | 8,155 |
| 1977 | 69,143 | 73,711 | -4,568 |
| 1978 | 91,878 | 91,144 | 734 |
| 1979 | 157,988 | 148,345 | 9,643 |
| 1980 | 128,950 | 139,227 | -10,277 |
| 1981 | 114,553 | 100,194 | 14,359 |
| 1982 | 289,319 | 275,360 | 13,959 |
| 1983 | 163,686 | 176,535 | -12,849 |
| 1984 | 142,882 | 142,182 | 700 |
| 1985 | 408,849 | 341,466 | 67,383 |
| 1986 | 196,890 | 241,781 | -44,891 |
| 1987 | 170,290 | 178,197 | -7,907 |
| 1988 | 367,176 | 351,044 | 16,132 |
| 1989 | 129,155 | 169,093 | -39,938 |
| 1990 | 126,095 | 118,444 | 7,651 |
| 1991 | 355,842 | 287,951 | 67,891 |
| 1992 | 153,483 | 147,097 | 6,386 |
| 1993 | 206,615 | 135,329 | 71,286 |
| 1994 | 294,146 | 246,536 | 47,610 |
| 1995 | 163,485 | 140,117 | 23,368 |
| 1996 | 183,662 | 180,076 | 3,586 |
| 1997 | 267,338 | 185,079 | 82,259 |
| 1998 | 183,180 | 178,562 | 4,618 |
| 1999 | 209,414 | 180,798 | 28,616 |

## Appendix 5: IPSA world congresses, 1950-1997

1    Zurich, Switzerland, Sep 4-9 1950; chair, local organising committee: Prof de Salis; programme chair: IPSA president Quincy Wright; theme: none; topics: 3; total papers: 8; participants, 81; countries represented, 23

2    Hague, Netherlands, Sep 8-12 1952; chair, local organising committee: M van Riel; programme chair: IPSA president Quincy Wright; theme: none; topics: 4; total papers: 57; participants, 220; countries represented, 31

3    Stockholm, Sweden, Aug 21-27 1955; chair, local organising committee: Gunnar Heckscher; programme chair: IPSA president William A Robson; theme: none; topics: 5; total papers: 25; participants, 275; countries represented, 36

4    Rome, Italy, Sep 16-20 1958; chair, local organising committee: Francesco Vito; programme chair: IPSA president James Pollock; theme: none; topics: 6; total papers: 77; participants, 320; countries represented, 31

5    Paris, France, Sep 26-30 1961; chair, local organising committee: Jean-Jacques Chevalier; programme chair: IPSA president Jacques Chapsal; theme: none; topics: 5; total papers: 59; participants, 425; countries represented, 46

6    Geneva, Switzerland, Sep 21-25 1964; chair, local organising committee: Rolland Ruffieux; programme chair: IPSA president DN Chester; theme: none; topics: 6; specialist meetings: 6; total papers: 94; participants, 494; countries represented, 43

7    Brussels, Belgium, Sep 18-23 1967; chair, local organising committee: Marcel Grégoire; programme chair: IPSA president Jacques Freymond; theme: none; topics: 9; specialist meetings: 10; total papers: 146; participants, 745; countries represented, 56

8    Munich, Germany, Aug 31-Sep 5 1970; local organising committee: Hans Maier, Kurt Sontheimer and Wolfgang Quint; programme chair: IPSA president Carl J Friedrich; theme: none; topics: 4; specialist meetings: 15; total papers: 259; participants, 894; countries represented, 46

9    Montreal, Canada, Aug 20-25 1973; chair, local organising committee: John Trent; programme chair: IPSA president Stein Rokkan; themes: (1) *Politics between economy and culture* (Stein Rokkan), (2) *Key issues in international conflict and peace research* (Karl Deutsch); main theme topics: 24; meetings of research committees: 7; specialist meetings: 12; total papers: 324; participants, 1,044; countries represented, 56

10   Edinburgh, United Kingdom, Aug 16-21 1976; programme chair: IPSA president Jean Laponce; theme: *Time, space and politics*; main theme topics: 22; meetings of research committees and study groups: 10; other meetings: 32; total papers: 327; participants, 1,081; countries represented, 56

11    Moscow, USSR, Aug 12-18 1979; secretary, local organising committee: William Smirnov; programme chair: Richard Merritt; theme: *Peace, development, knowledge: contributions of political science*; main theme topics: 57; meetings of research committees and study groups: 43; other meetings: 38; total papers: 450; participants, 1,466; countries represented, 53

12    Rio de Janeiro, Brazil, Aug 9-14 1982; local organisers: Martha P de Moraes and Christina Castello; programme chair: Guillermo O'Donnell; theme: *Society beyond the state in the 1980s*; subthemes: 3; main theme sessions: 54; meetings of research committees and study groups: 33; other meetings: 28; total papers: approx. *825*; participants, 1,477; countries represented, 49

13    Paris, France, Jul 15-20 1985; local organiser: Serge Hurtig; programme chair: Francesco Kjellberg; theme: *The changing state and its interaction with national and international society*; subthemes: 4; main theme sessions: 103; meetings of research committees and study groups: 99; other meetings: 79; total papers: *approx. 600*; participants, 1,763; countries represented, 66

14    Washington, USA, Aug 28-Sep 1 1988; local organiser: Robert Hauck; programme chair: Harold K Jacobson; theme: *Toward a global political science*; main theme sessions: 91; meetings of research committees and study groups: 79; other meetings: 62; total papers: approx. 890; participants, 1,265; countries represented, 74

15    Buenos Aires, Argentina, Jul 21-25 1991; chair, local organising committee: Oscar Oszlak; programme chair: Jean Leca; theme: *Centres and peripheries in contemporary politics: Interdependence and power asymmetries*; subthemes: 4; main theme sessions: 68; meetings of research committees and study groups: 105; other meetings: 46; total papers: approx. 870; participants, approx. 1,400; countries represented, approx. 55

16    Berlin, Germany, Aug 21-25 1994; chair, local organising committee: Gerhard Göhler; programme chair: Robert Goodin; theme: *Democratisation*; subthemes: 8; main theme sessions: 57; meetings of research committees and study groups: 79; other meetings: 86; total papers: approx. 660; participants, 1,884; countries represented, 73

17    Seoul, Korea, Aug 17-21 1997; chair, local organising committee: Dalchoong Kim; programme chair: I William Zartman; theme: *Conflict and Order*; subthemes: 5; main theme sessions: 41; meetings of research committees and study groups: 92; other meetings: 92; total papers: 110; participants, 1,470; countries represented, 72

## Appendix 6: IPSA roundtable meetings, 1952-1999

| 1. 1952 | Apr 6-10 | Cambridge | The teaching of political science |
| 2. 1953 | Aug 10-12 | Paris | Comparative public administration |
| 3. 1954 | Apr 5-10 | Florence | Teaching and research in comparative government |
| 4. 1956 | Sep 10-16 | La-Tour-de Peilz | Political representation of farmers; the doctrine of peaceful coexistence; new methods and techniques in political science |
| 5. 1957 | Sep 10-13 | Pittsburgh | Pressure groups |
| 6. 1959 | Sep 1-5 | Opatija | Civil military relations in the modern state; political science in Europe |
| 7. 1960 | Sep 12-15 | Ann Arbor | Recent developments in the study of political behaviour; problems of polyethnic states |
| 8. 1962 | Sep 11-12 | Freudenstadt | The political role of the courts; constitutionalism |
| 9. 1963 | Sep 18-23 | Oxford | Federalism; decentralisation |
| 10. 1965 | Sep 13-17 | Grenoble | Opposition and control: problems and perspectives; the political role of international economic organisations |
| 11. 1966 | Sep 18-24 | Jablonna | Political aspects of economic organisations; problems of representation |
| 12. 1968 | Sep 16-20 | Salzburg | Modernisation of political decision making processes; political problems of planning |
| 13. 1969 | Sep 10-14 | Turin | Comparative European politics; political decision making |
| 14. 1971 | Sep 15-18 | Louvain | Key issues of peace research; politics of economic integration in Europe, East and West |
| 15. 1972 | Sep 12-15 | Bucharest | Democracy and information; political independence and economic co-operation |
| 16. 1974 | Sep 9-13 | Jerusalem | Political integration: conceptualisation, configurational-analytic cross-polity comparison |

| 17. 1975 | Sep 9-14 | Dubrovnik | Participation and self-management as factors in the transformation of contemporary political systems; class interests and national interests |
| 18. 1977 | Aug 29-Sep 3 | Krakow | Political culture and political development |
| 19. 1978 | Aug 25-27 | Rio de Janeiro | Technocracy and its controls |
| 20. 1979 | Nov 25-28 | Calcutta | Non-alignment |
| 21. 1980 | Aug 25-26 | Weimar | Detente: reasons, demands, obstacles |
| 22. 1981 | Jan 8-9 | Zurich | International crises and crisis management |
| 23. 1982 | Mar 29-Apr 1 | Tokyo | The new international economic order and political development in the Asian-Pacific region |
| 24. 1983 | Sep 6-8 | Urbana-Champaign | Global communication |
| 25. 1984 | Apr 3-4 | Florence | Government under pressure: the capacity of government to cope with urgent social problems |
| 26. 1985 | Mar 15-16 | Zagreb | Interest and politics |
| 27. 1986 | Mar 10-11 | Buenos Aires | Democratisation processes in comparative perspective |
| 28. 1986 | Oct 2-4 | Ottawa | The crisis in political thought: towards a renewal |
| 29. 1987 | Apr 6-7 | Berlin (East) | New approaches to political thinking in view of global issues |
| 30. 1988 | Mar 23-25 | Moscow | Global modelling and political science |
| 31. 1989 | Aug 24-26 | Oslo | Modernisation of the public sector: dealing with problems of efficiency and legitimacy |
| 32. 1990 | May 22-24 | Seoul | The state, politics and economy: causal relations |
| 33. 1991 | Apr 22-23 | Warsaw | Transition to democracy in Eastern Europe: a comparative perspective |
| 34. 1992 | Jan 27-31 | Madras | Democracy and social tensions in third world countries |
| 35. 1992 | Sep 3-5 | Chicago | Political science and the study of global environmental change |
| 36. 1994 | Mar 25-27 | Kyoto | International order and domestic political economy in the post-cold |

|        |          |                |                                                    |
|--------|----------|----------------|----------------------------------------------------|
|        |          |                | war system: implications for the Asia-Pacific region |
| 37. 1995 | Jan 15-16 | Taipei       | Divided nations in a comparative perspective       |
| 38. 1995 | Aug 28-29 | Prague       | The relationship between politics and economics: an important condition for the stability of the state |
| 39. 1996 | Apr 26   | Oslo           | The politics of sustainable development            |
| 40. 1997 | Mar 4-5  | Rio de Janeiro | Division of powers as a challenge in contemporary democracies |
| 41. 1998 | Feb 12-13 | Quebec        | Integration and disintegration: new partnerships in the world order |
| 42. 1999 | Apr 27   | Krakow         | Convergence or confrontation: can western democratic capitalism be a global pattern? |
| 43. 1999 | Oct 7-10 | Ercolano       | Scientific communication in the year 2000 and beyond |
| 44. 2000 | Feb 25   | Be'er Sheva    | Regional conflicts and their resolution            |

# INDEX